THE CONSPIRACY to DESTROY
BLACK WOMEN

MICHAEL PORTER

Front Cover Illustration by Tony Quaid

First Edition

Third Printing

Copyright © 2001 by Michael Porter

10-Digit ISBN #: 0913543721
13-Digit ISBN #: 978-0913543726

This book is dedicated to my grandmother, Dorothy Booker; my mother, Evelyn Porter; my sisters, Debra, Jackie, and Gina; and my niece, Tammy.

CONTENTS

Introduction

Women and men of all races who are committed to revolutionary feminist movement, who want to end sexism and sexist exploitation and oppression, recognize that we create and sustain the conditions for solidarity and coalition building by vigilantly challenging the ethic of competition, replacing it with a communal ethic of collective benefit.

bell hooks' *Killing Rage: Ending Racism*
(bell hooks spells her name with lower case letters.)

Woman, Mother—your responsibility is one that might make angels tremble and fear to take hold!

Anna J. Cooper's *A Voice in the South*

INTRODUCTION

Why did I, an African American man, write this book? Allow me to explain several experiences that heightened my awareness of the lives and the plight of women, particularly African American women. My maternal grandmother is 89 years of age. She's mentally sharp. During one of my many conversations with my grandmother I became angry—not at my grandmother but at a White supremacist social structure that kept this brilliant woman from becoming the mathematician or engineer we always felt she should have become. Grandma, you see, is a mathematical genius! I don't know, maybe it's a strange kind of naiveté, but I hurt when I see positive human potential denied, suppressed, and crushed. Fortunately, however, my grandmother is the embodiment of spiritual strength. My mother, too, experienced the racist societal mechanism of checkmating African American women. My pain persisted.

When I was an educational therapist for the Charter Corporation during the early '80s, I attended a seminar on eating disorders—anorexia nervosa and bulimia. Several prominent White psychiatrists conducted the seminar. They stated that there were no documented cases of African American women suffering from eating disorders. I knew that every eating disorder patient in the adolescent component were White females from middle and upper class families. Today, however, it is not uncommon for African American females to suffer from anorexia nervosa or bulimia.

The proverbial 'straw that broke the camel's back' occurred while I was a child and adolescent therapist for the state of Georgia. This experience was twofold. First, I could not determine the reason one of my bright middle school female clients would either skip school or fake an illness in order to go home. During a visit to her at school, she told me that the other students always called her "black." She then told me that she hates herself. A few days later I was conducting a self-image program for African American teens and young adults. I held up two pictures—one of a light complexioned African American woman and the other of a dark complexioned African American woman. I asked, "Which do you consider to be pretty?" The picture of the light complexioned woman was unanimously chosen.

So, why did I write this book? Maybe to help stop the mental, emotional, and spiritual bleeding of African American women; or maybe to help ease my pain, which is forever connected to the plight of African American women. As the saying goes, "We're all in the same boat." As an oppressed African man, I cannot fall for the lie that only men will bring about self-determination for oppressed people. We're all in the same boat.

Women catch hell. Women catch hell because they

are born into a social-political-economic system that is owned and operated by patriarchal White male supremacists. Although there are some dysfunctional African American, Latino, Native American, and poor White men, they are not the problem. Nonwhite manhood is absolutely discouraged under White male supremacy. These oppressed men are missocialized and, in the case of nonwhite men, miseducated to be dysfunctional. The problem is the patriarchal White male supremacist who uses his military, economic, and political power to subjugate people of color under his control. As a result of this control, women catch hell.

The patriarchal White power structure has deemed women the playthings of the world. Women are missocialized to entertain men, and men are miseducated and missocialized to view women as their entertainment. It does not stop at entertainment. Men are also miseducated and missocialized to abuse and pimp women. This entire demonic process unfolds from girlhood to womanhood, seriously hindering women from becoming self-determined. Self-determination is something the patriarchal White power structure absolutely does not want women to possess. As most women realize, they are in for the fight of their lives. They must challenge both the patriarchal White supremacist and their own miseducated, missocialized men.

The Conspiracy to Destroy Black Women provides a no-nonsense approach and perspective to fight patriarchal White male supremacist oppression. This book is not anti-male; it is anti-female oppression. Those who gain from the oppression of women do not want their victims to understand that when women are oppressed, so are their families and communities. When mother is crucified, her children die too. If economically, educationally, spiritually oppressed communities are to become productive, mothers must become empowered. Many women are home alone and too many African American and Latino men are on the new slave plantation (prisons). The situation is too severe for women to simply suffer and wait for their men to lead them to victory. Patriarchal White supremacy is too deadly for women to simply pray and hope that it goes away. Women must unite and fight.

This book offers insight into the how and why of female oppression in America, and perhaps the world. The beliefs, philosophies, and morals of the patriarchal White male power structure are examined in a no-nonsense, cause-effect manner. And although some may believe that all women should be lumped together simply because of their womanhood, I did not hesitate to focus on philosophical and other differences that exist in the lives of women—especially racial differences. Such a realistic focus is nec-essary in assisting women to become self-determining.

Although written to assist women, oppressed men should read and discuss this book. Oppressed men are not members of the patriarchal White power structure, and must, therefore, comprehend the dynamics of female oppression and its effect on families, communities, and themselves. Oppression is seldom an isolated event or condition. It spreads throughout groups of people. Even superficial examination would reveal the domino aspect of oppression.

For the past 500 years, the face of the oppressor has been that of the White male. White men rule, and they rule with a bloodletting vengeance. Works such as Frances Cress Welsing's *The Isis Papers*, bell hooks' *Killing Rage: Ending Racism* and *Black Looks: Race and Representation*, Marimba Ani's *Yurugu*, Angela Y. Davis' *Women, Race & Class*, Amos N. Wilson's *Black on Black Violence*, and Cheikh

Anta Diop's *African Origins* must be used as survival study guides by the victims of patriarchal White supremacy. As global economic conditions worsen for the world's workers, and America's population becomes more nonwhite, we will experience a renewed spirit of ruthlessness from the White male power structure. And be not deceived: single, working, and elderly women will suffer tremendously.

Homicide is the leading cause of death for pregnant women. Past studies had erroneously classified these deaths as maternal deaths due to bleeding and infection. More women are also battered during their pregnancy.

Mother is nailed to the cross of patriarchal White male supremacy, and we are all obligated to rescue her. If she's not rescued then we all will die and, God forbid, may be condemned to hell—the consequence of not attempting to fulfill our obligation to Mother.

The heart of a woman falls back with the night,
And enters some alien cage in its plight,
And tries to forget it has dreamed of the stars,
While it breaks, breaks, breaks on the sheltering bars.
                Georgia D. Johnson's *The Heart Of A Woman*

PART ONE

CAUSE, EFFECT, AND MADNESS

CHAPTER 1

WHEN LOVE HURTS:
SPOUSE ABUSE AND SEXUAL MOLESTATION

While working as a child and family therapist, I had the opportunity to help many families deal with issues of domestic violence—verbal and physical abuse of the female spouse and sexual molestation of the children. In my practice I've found that insecurities, the use of control, fear to assure loyalty, and the displacement of anger were the reasons men battered their wives. Morally unrestrained, lustful perversion was the primary dynamic in the molestation of female children. Ironically, these dynamics are also active in the patriarchal White male supremacist power structure. Consequently, American society does not embrace trusting, patient, secure male-female relationships.

Insecurity, control, and anger displacement arise when White men experience job loss, financial setbacks, diminished social status, or sexual impotence. Feelings of love for the wife are selfishly based on the husband's material status and his view of adequate sexual functioning (which is not necessarily the wife's view). If the husband is financially satisfied, then he is able to "love" his wife; if not, he cannot be satisfied or love his wife. Quite often, when the husband has no money, the woman is wrongfully accused of acting differently. Thus, the husband's feelings of insecurity gradually move toward displacement of anger. A man believes that if he loses his money, he'll lose control or influence over his wife. The dangerous logic is that women can be purchased and that if all else fails (meaning the husband's control), physical violence will set things right. So the wife is physically beaten.

Remember, this same logic is inherent in the White male supremacist power structure: *If all else fails, kill or injure the opponent.*

Let's now examine some of the spouse abuse dynamics that exist within many African American men. Unfortunately, many African American men are very familiar with issues of unemployment and underemployment; therefore, job loss is *not always* an issue in African American men abusing their wives. Some miseducated African American men who consider themselves "players" are sexually active with both their wives and a girlfriend. Several clients have stated that they can get sex from a woman even if they don't have a penny in their pockets. Such logic points to a dynamic that is different from White males.

The dynamic existing among too many African American men (many of our boys too) is what I call the charisma factor: The belief that charm, attitude, and persuasive speech compel women to desire their company. From my experience, some African American men become physically abusive of their spouse when they feel they no longer possess the charisma factor. The charisma factor is *very fragile!* The following female behaviors and actions can trigger extreme feelings of insecurity and rage in some African American men:

- A perceived show of disrespect.
- A change in dinner preparation routine.
- A visit to her mother's home.
- A visit to a female friend's house.
- A smile from a former male school mate. Some men respond by slapping, punching, kicking, strangling, stabbing, cussing, or drawing a gun on their wives and girl friends.

The control dynamic has entered at this point. If charisma fails, then force must prevail. Of course, the wife is blamed for this destructive behavior (anger displacement). Let's examine a case in point.

The August/September 2000 issue of *Heart & Soul* magazine features a painfully revealing article entitled "Behind Closed Doors: Living a Life of Abuse." The article explains Lola's loving relationship with Kevin. As long as Lola was dependent upon Kevin (both are African American) the relationship went well, but after Lola enrolled in college, Kevin began to physically abuse her. It is my belief that Kevin felt threatened by Lola's desire to better herself in a way that he could not control, and he attempted to regain control through inflicting violence upon Lola. In sad and sick fashion, insecure African American men *need* someone to control; this need makes it impossible to have healthy, growth-oriented relationships with women. The article mentions research from the Emory University School of Medicine which states that half of African American women who have attempted to commit suicide reported being abused.[1] Perhaps even scarier is the fact that, according to the U.S. Department of Justice, African American women, women living in urban areas, and women living in low-income households experience high rates of domestic violence.[2]

African American men, as do African American women, live under a constant threat to our very humanity, and if there is no spiritual grounding or racial awareness—in an African-centered sense—pathologically destructive behaviors will result, as is seen in domestic violence. As relates to White men and women, they are (collectively speaking) superiority and materially based; spirituality is nonexistent or irrelevant in their scheme of things. Their existence is deemed worthy only if they believe themselves to be better than other humans and if they have accumulated large sums of money.

When a man physically or verbally abuses a woman, he is asserting his belief that the woman is inferior. Some men know that they may face harsh legal consequences for hitting their wives or girlfriends, but they cannot stop themselves. It is quite possible that some abusive men may develop sadistic traits; they may begin to enjoy abusing their mates. Again, we must acknowledge that sadistic behavior is woven into the fabric of the patriarchal White power structure. We are socialized to enjoy viewing violence and this enjoyment is, at times, transformed into a desire to actually *do* the violence. And who better to inflict violence against than a class of individuals society has deemed *the weaker sex*? If women don't raise hell, I don't see an end to spouse abuse. Victims must save themselves. Too many women put up with physical, emotional, and verbal abuse because they fear losing their husbands' salaries or being murdered by the husband. Some believe they don't deserve better. As a result, these women will remain quiet about their tormented lives until the signs of abuse become all too clear. These economic and psycho-emotional aspects of abuse must be thoroughly addressed in helping women to free themselves from all types of abuse. Let us now explore sexual abuse of female girls.

When men sexually molest female children they have given in to a base, morally unchecked desire to experience sex with someone they can conquer. The female child is a guinea pig for the male's lustful desires; he can enjoy the "newness" of the child, and he can do as he pleases with her and avoid any negative consequences (avoidance achieved through instilling fear into the child

victim). He can have sex with someone who's pure, innocent, and controllable. Under patriarchal White supremacy,
females are attacked shortly after leaving their mother's
womb. This society only superficially advocates the teaching of moral discipline. The primary, motivating value is
to do whatever feels good. Thus, we have what is essentially the rhetorical ethic that Marimba Ani explains in
*Yurugu: An African-Centered Critique of European Cul-
tural Thought and Behavior:* There's no reason to feel
guilty or ashamed about having your way with others, including children. Women, along with men of conscience,
must protect their children at all cost. In a morally corrupt society in which sexual freedom really means doing
whatever you want as long as you can get away with it,
women must protect themselves and their daughters. Some
young female victims of sexual abuse will survive, such
as the multi-talented Oprah Winfrey, but many will battle
the emotional and psychological turmoil the rest of their
lives. The message, "open season on females is over,"
must be transmitted through example, not rhetoric. Everything from physically incapacitating the abuser to push-
ing for stronger punishment through legislation must be
undertaken by women. Only then will this pathological
behavior end.

CHAPTER 2

BITCH, HOE, OR QUEEN?
THE ROLE OF WOMEN IN RAP MUSIC AND VIDEOS

Only in a morally bankrupt society would one find popular, for-profit, generally accepted, and blatant exploitation of women in the media. Although such exploitation exists in television programs and Hollywood movies, it has become pervasive in rap videos and rap music. Before going further, understand a major point: Teenagers and young adults are the major audience for rap music and videos. They are being desensitized to exploitation while being conditioned to *love* and *enjoy* the exploitation of women *without even knowing that this is being done to them*! This is the perverted genius of the patriarchal White male supremacist power structure—people are programmed just like computers. The result is that this society has ten-year-old boys believing it's "cool" to call girls bitch, freak, skeezer, and hoe. Too many girls, and even some women, accept being called derogatory names. In her book *Ladies First: Revelations of a Strong Woman*, Queen Latifah states:

> I'm writing this book to let every woman know that
> she, too—no matter what her status or place in life—
> is royalty. This is particularly important for African
> American women to know inside and out, upside
> down, and right side up. For so long in this society,
> we have been given—and have allowed ourselves
> to take—the role of slave, concubine, mammy,
> second-class citizen, bitch, hoe. Many of us have
> been so hurt and so dogged out by society—and
> by men and by life—that we can't even wrap our
> brains around the notion that we deserve better,
> that we are queens.[1]

It has been said that if you call a person a name long enough she or he will begin to believe it. Imagine if teenage males and females were conditioned and encouraged to address one another as queen and king, and to *act* like royalty! Women will claim their rightful place on this planet only when they begin to see themselves as sacred creations. Latifah states that women were created in "Her image."[2] Unfortunately, the rap industry tends to shun positive messages put forth by such women as Sister Souljah and others because positive rap is a threat to the patriarchal White male power structure. The power structure understands the necessity of keeping us happy, violent, and lustful. Watching and listening to destructive lyrics serves this end. The victims of White supremacy must remain ignorant if the White supremacist is to remain in power. Sister Souljah, alone, scared the hell out of the White male power structure with her consciousness raising lyrics! Unfortunately, most rap music and videos that get air and television time portray females as lust-crazed, money-hungry worshipers of foul-mouthed male generated filth.

Popularity and wealth are promised to African American males (sadly, some female rap artists participate in the madness) who are willing to call women names and glorify doing all sorts of sadistic sexual acts to women. Put a funky beat to disrespectful lyrics and abracadabra! It's a chart busting hit! Too often the music industry, as well as other industries under the White male power structure, pimps women and girls. I believe that young girls watching rap videos develop two destructive beliefs: They begin to view themselves as unattractive if they don't resemble the half naked, made up, light skinned females with long hair in the videos; and they begin to believe that it's alright for boys and men to treat women like toys, especially if the boy or man has an expensive car and money—all she has to do is provide the sex. Under patriarchal White male supremacy, every act is driven by profits. Understand: Women and girls *are the product* of rap music and videos. The "bitch" is tied to money, the "hoe" is tied to money, the "freak" is tied to money, and the "bait" is tied to money. Several scenarios provide examples. A teenage male starches his most expensive jeans, buys the latest Jordans, and goes to a fine department store to purchase the latest Hilfiger shirt to match his jeans so that he can look "fresh" for the "bitches" or "them hoes." A well educated, professional male puts on his Brooks Brothers suit to go to a local hangout so that he can "score" with a female. I personally believe that men and boys seek women and girls that closely resemble those in rap videos—they desire the *product*. Women are not to be protected, loved, and respected, but are to be *purchased* and *used*.

Women must protest the blatant, wholesale exploitation of women. Women must critique the rap songs their children listen to. Women must monitor and boycott rap videos that exploit women. Women must protest rap concerts that feature violent, exploitative rap artists. Women must sponsor, purchase products, and otherwise support those female rap artists that are about liberation. Women must challenge the wickedly clever argument that these destructive videos and songs are "art." Women must challenge African American rap artists about exploiting their own people. The role of women in rap music and videos must be changed from negative to positive. I recommend that women call, write, and e-mail all stations that offend them.

Second, involve the entire family and have your children and husband also express their dissatisfaction.

CHAPTER 3

SBF

Single Black Female. It is well known that more than half of all African American households are headed by single women and/or grandmothers. Thank God for the grandmothers. The problems facing African Americans would be worse if it were not for grandmothers, elderly grandmothers, rearing their grandchildren or helping their daughters rear the children. Where are the Brothers/fathers? Let's examine several dynamics which seriously influence African American female-male relations. These dynamics have given rise to the existence of single African American motherhood.

Question: How is it that in some African and Asian countries, women and men marry, and remain married, to a virtual stranger who was chosen for them by their families? The answer is, because they live under a different value system. Even though the tenacles of White supremacy reach far and wide, some nonwhite cultures have been able to hold on to ancient, historical customs and values that predate colonialism and the European slave trade. I have several African friends who never met their wives until both families had decided on a particular woman. In America, we are "free" to date and marry the person of our choice, but most of our relationships fail! Something is seriously wrong, and that "something" is the value system developed by patriarchal White supremacy.

Our "freedom" to choose a mate is not true freedom because we live within an alien society and its destructive belief system. Jawanza Kunjufu has stated that we choose our clothes and cars better than we choose our mates. The Brother is correct. Under patriarchal White supremacy, we are conditioned to like someone who makes us "feel good." An examination of beliefs, attitudes, and behaviors is, if done at all, only superficial. And men have it worst of all. Under this wicked value system, men are conditioned to "love" women based on facial "beauty," hair, breasts, behinds, legs, thighs, and women's willingness to let men enjoy these "assets." This is extreme perversion, and is, therefore, illogical. It really makes no damn sense! It is common to hear a man say, in response to being questioned about his love for a woman, that, "I love the way she looks and the way she makes me feel." Lust is often mistaken for love. Under patriarchal White supremacy, most healthy values are turned upside down and the people become confused as a result. These values are not even working for White families, and they have a built-in safety net under patriarchal White supremacy.

This diabolical system encourages women to attract men with their body parts. Women are encouraged to use looks to obtain a mate, especially a mate with a "good" job. This excludes many hard working Brothers who are janitors, truck drivers, mechanics, and cooks. As a result, men are attracted to what women reveal to them—pretty faces and attractive bodies. After becoming accustomed to his woman's body, too many men eventually turn their attention to the body of another woman. This is a sick game of man meets woman; man has sex with woman; man becomes disinterested with woman; man seeks and meets another woman; man leaves broken hearts and lonely children along the way. Such madness usually takes place after a very superficial dating game in which both men and women avoid serious discussion, and manifest little, if any, patience before becoming sexually intimate.

The so-called romance of a relationship is illusional. We go to movies, walk through the park, tell jokes, send flowers, and then we have sex and fall out. American society has taught us to act like this. This is how Hollywood does it. This is how soap operas do it. This is how recording artists sing about it. But such a way of believing and behaving is not healthy, nor is it realistic. Our so-called freedom to choose is, in reality, a destructive, programmed way of thinking and acting. Under patriarchal White supremacy, we are little more than Skinner's rat and Pavlov's dog—conditioned by various means to believe and respond in a predetermined manner. The goal: to confuse and divide us for the sole purpose of maintaining our victim status under patriarchal White supremacy.

The social/racist dynamic must be equally, if not more, understood by women. Dr. Frances Cress Welsing states:

> The dynamic of white genetic survival necessitates the destruction of the Black male. White supremacy brings the image of the Black male down to nothing. For example, 99 percent of the Black men on the evening news have handcuffs on their wrists. The Black male's functioning is further undermined by the absence of jobs and opportunities. The Black man is attacked because he can cause white genetic annihilation. After the Black man is attacked, it becomes almost impossible for him to be the breadwinner. The female has to move in and become the breadwinner, as well as the family's emotional support.[1]

It is little wonder that divorce is so prevalent and that so many African American women are having to go to court to force men, who once loved their fine bodies, to now pay child support. Many of these Brothers who have difficulty paying child support were once able to squeeze out enough money for movies, hotels, and anything else that made it easier to get sex from a woman. These totally mixed up priorities often lead many African American men to their first jail lock-up. It is a cruel and vicious cycle—lust/then hatred/then children/then jail.

White men have no use for African men. Sure, we play sports, sing, dance, act, and hold some professional positions, but don't be deceived into believing that the Black man is accepted with open arms. African American males only serve to keep White males wealthy and powerful through our roles as athletes in white-owned teams, singers, and actors in White-owned production companies, and inmates in private, state, and federal prisons. We even serve in death for White-owned coffin makers. The patriarchal White supremacists' educational system is, for African American males, a *mis*educational system. We are not taught to own and operate banks and other businesses and to provide opportunities for our people. This, African American women must understand, is the reality of African American manhood under patriarchal White supremacy. And this seriously impacts African American female-male relations.

Men feel good when they can financially contribute to their households. Men love being able to provide their wives and children with houses, cars, and other necessities of modern living. I have counseled too many frustrated, angry, and depressed African American men who were unable to substantially contribute to their households. Believe me, this is no light concern. Families fall apart because of men feeling inadequate as the head of household.

The dynamic of materialism in American society places extreme stress on African male victims of White supremacy. This stress serves the dual function of destroying African families and strengthening patriarchal White supremacy. Extreme materialism causes people to view

14

potential mates from a monetary perspective only. This is not good. If a woman only seeks a man with a substantial income and fails to examine his beliefs, attitudes, and values, she has set herself up for failure. She will, in essence, become another one of his purchases; he purchased her and now he owns her. Money is good to have, but it does not make the man. It is better to have a man who is willing to legitimately support his family spiritually and economically, even if it means throwing newspapers seven days a week, than to have a banker who abuses women. It is better to have a man who knows how to manage and grow his money than one who spends beyond his means. Many persons with substantial incomes are in great debt because of their excessive spending and poor saving habits.

For many African American males, the end result of financial frustration is the new slave plantation called prison. With more African American males in prison than in college, there promises to be some rough days ahead for African American female-male relationships. We are victims of a false freedom in choosing mates, and we are victims of a vicious, racist social structure. Awareness and acknowledgment of this problem are necessary. We must believe we can form healthy relationships. Healthy African American female-male relationships will give us power—the power to become self-determining as an African family.

CHAPTER 4

AIDS AND AFRICAN/AFRICAN AMERICAN WOMEN
"Jesus wept."
John 11:35

African/African American women are overwhelmingly dying from the plague. The plague is the Acquired Immune Deficiency Syndrome (AIDS). What was once called the gay White man's disease is now taking the lives of African/African American women in record numbers. When it comes to AIDS deaths, the Sisters in North America and Africa have a common bond of death.

> Sub-Saharan Africa continues to bear the brunt of HIV and AIDS, with close to 70% of the global total of HIV positive people. Most will die in the next 10 years, joining the 13.7 million Africans already claimed by the epidemic and leaving behind shattered families and crippled prospects for development.[1]

This is both tragic and scary. During various conversations among African Americans, we sometimes pose the hypothetical question, "What will the world be like without Black people?"

A ghastly possible answer may be revealed here:

> Because of AIDS, companies doing business in Africa are hurting and are bracing themselves for far worse as their workers die. According to a survey of commercial farmers in Kenya, illness and death have already replaced old-age retirement as the leading reason why employees leave service. Retirement accounted for just 2% of employee drop-out by 1997. Life expectancy at birth in southern Africa, which rose from 44 years in the early

1950s to 59 in the early 1990s, is set to drop to just 45 between 2005 and 2010 because of AIDS. In contrast, South Asians, who could barely reach their 40th birthday in 1950, can expect by 2005 to be living 22 years longer than their counterparts in AIDS-ravaged Africa.[2]

It is possible for the more than one billion African people in the global diaspora (Africa, Brazil, the U.S., the Caribbean, and Europe) to drastically dwindle to mere millions because of AIDS related deaths. In Africa, 13 women are infected for every 10 men.[3] Across the Atlantic, African American women comprise 60 percent of new AIDS cases, with an AIDS rate 16 times that of White women (61.9 compared to 3.8 per 100,000 population).[4] We, all African people, are in trouble. Sure, we've been in trouble for almost 600 years but this problem is wiping us out across the planet.

Further complicating matters for African American women is the fact that at least 38 percent of new AIDS cases are contracted through heterosexual means.[5] The love of a woman's life may lead to the loss of her life. Bisexuality among African American men must be examined. Many African American ministers, politicians, and men of various professions are gay or bisexual—**and married** (as are many White men). Many professional gay/bisexual men marry for social reasons (e.g., ministers are expected to have wives). Some women don't know that their men are gay/bisexual. Some naive women have the bizarre belief that they can change their men's sexual orientation. Besides the frustration of sleeping with a man who wishes that he was sleeping with *his* man, there is the possibility that he or his male partner is having unsafe sex.

Then there are the drugs, heroin and crack cocaine. Here the dynamics are simple: Crack and heroin addicts can't keep jobs long, and must resort to selling their bodies, among other crimes, in order to fund their habits. Heroin addicts often share needles, thus passing HIV along. Some crack or heroin addicted men, too, sell their bodies, generally to homosexual men. Some men with wives or girlfriends sleep with crack addicted female prostitutes. It is truly a scary situation.

And then there are the Brothers on America's new slave plantations, also known as prisons. Though the data is vague on how many incarcerated African American males are HIV positive, there is general agreement that the number is growing. I believe that state and federal authorities know that a wide-spread panic would result if accurate HIV/AIDS numbers on incarcerated men were released. Does the incidence of HIV and AIDS among incarcerated African American males mean that most of these Brothers are homosexuals? No, it does not. As gut wrenching as this may sound, there are punks and homosexuals in prison. Punks are heterosexual men who are either raped by other men or who engage in sexual activity with one man in order to prevent being raped by groups of men. Homosexuals are just that: Homosexuals. The reasons for this behavior among imprisoned men must be studied in depth, but the effect of this behavior on African American women is obvious: Many of these brothers return home to girlfriends and wives. Women whose men have served prison time should go with them and have them tested, straight up! Women should lovingly tell their man, we are doing this for us and our future children. If he refuses, again lovingly tell him you love yourself too much to act irresponsibly. Most men I've counseled are embarrassed to state that they were raped or that they voluntarily had sex with one or two men to prevent being raped. Brothers who raped other men are not likely to tell their mates. Having them tested for HIV is the safest and smart thing to do.

What can African/African American women do to save themselves? How does White supremacy factor into this gloomy scenario?

> Researchers and service providers need a better understanding of the role of cultural and socio-economic factors in the transmission of HIV, as well as the effect of racial inequality on public health. In addition, public health officials should consider changing epidemiological surveillance to include other demographic information such as social, economic and cultural factors. These efforts need to influence the design of HIV prevention messages, services and programs. [6]

In order to significantly reduce the spread of AIDS among African/African American women, an honest look at the effects of White supremacist oppression on all African lives is absolutely necessary. The effects of African colonization and American slavery and racism on Sisters must be further studied.

First, a revolution in the beliefs and behaviors of all African people is necessary to stop the madness of AIDS. A people who are encouraged by a patriarchal White supremacist social structure to engage in sex as a recreational activity are at high risk of contracting the AIDS virus. Women conditioned to believe that they must give sex in order to receive love are at high risk of contracting AIDS. Women and men who have been encouraged to stop being old-fashioned and to start engaging in sexual orgies and mate swapping (because White folk do it) are at high risk of contracting AIDS. There *must* be a revolution in the beliefs and behaviors of all African people if we are to reduce and survive the AIDS epidemic.

African/African American women must utilize any and all approaches, traditional and nontraditional, to saving their lives and our lives. Sisters living deep in the 'hood and in rural areas must be reached as well as those residing in luxurious suburbia. Sisters must also make men wait, *really wait*, before engaging in sexual activities with them. There is too much impatience in African American female-male relationships; we move too fast and end up suffering too much. Women must sit and seriously talk among themselves and with men about sexual activity and AIDS; straight to the point conversations must take place on a regular basis. Fear of talking is a luxury none of us can afford.

African/African American women must also work with political officials, schools and hospital administrators and board members to develop programs designed to decrease the number of African/African American women with AIDS. Expectations and timelines must be stated. The life and death urgency of the situation must be articulated by the women and felt by the officials and administrators. Racist medical practices, including racist attitudes, must be put on the table and dealt with. Elected officials at every level control the allocation of public funds; hospital administrators and board members control the allocation of hospital resources. The goal is affordable access to HIV treatment drugs such as Zidovudine (ZDV, also known as AZT), Zalcitabine (ddC), Didanosine (ddI), Lamivudine (3TC), Stavudine (d4T), and Nevirapine.

African/African American women must also seek to ease the psychological pain which is, on a daily basis, experienced by their people. I believe that much of this pain comes from frustrated, deferred dreams which leads to feelings of anger, depression, and hopelessness. Drugs such as alcohol, crack, and heroin are used as a means of escape from the pain. Sometimes sex is used as a means of escaping from psychological and emotional pain. Comprehending and dealing with these psychological-emotional stressors will prevent many African/African American women from engaging in drug use or sexual activity as a means of escape. Many of those currently using drugs or engaging in escapist sexual activity will stop when they learn how to effectively function and productively cope within a White supremacist social structure.

Now, let's look at what I believe is the cause of AIDS and the high AIDS rate among African/African American women.

> Medicine, if it means anything at all, means to ascertain the fundamental (rock bottom) causation of disease. Ultimately, the fundamental cause of a given disease determines what must be done about it. Otherwise, one is treating various symptoms of a disease. Sometimes a disease may be a symptom of something else. AIDS (Acquired Immune Deficiency Syndrome) is recognized as a disease, but AIDS may also be a *symptom* of yet another disease, which must be determined.[7]

Again, the cause of AIDS must be explained, understood, and accepted by African/African American women. In chapter 25 of *The Isis Papers*, psychiatrist Frances Cress Welsing, an African American woman, clearly explains that the AIDS epidemic is a premeditated chemical-biological warfare activity undertaken by the White supremacist power structure for the sole purpose of assuring White genetic survival through the population reduction of nonwhite people, especially African/African American people.[8] According to Dr. Welsing AIDS was presented to the world as an African disease caused by the African Green Monkey.[9] Quoting from *A Survey of Chemical and Biological Warfare*, by John Cookson and Judith Nottingham,

> The question of whether new diseases could be used is of considerable interest. Vervet monkey disease (African Green Monkey Disease) may well be an example of a whole new class of disease-causing organisms. Handling of blood and tissue without precaution causes infection. It is unaffected by any antibiotic substance so far tried and is unrelated to any other organism. It causes fatality in some cases and can be venerally transmitted in man. It has possible potential as an infectious disease of man. It presumably is also of BW (biological warfare) interest. New diseases are continually appearing. . . In addition to these there are the possibilities of virus and bacteria being genetically manipulated to produce 'new' organisms.[10]

A Survey of Chemical and Biological Warfare was published in 1969. Patriarchal White male supremacists are very efficient at perfecting ways to take human life. Many people are understandably frightened by how far White supremacy will go to maintain its domination of the earth. The Nazi regime's murder of 6,000,000 European Jews and the Tuskegee Syphilis Experiments (which lasted 40 years) in America are examples of how far patriarchal White supremacy will go. There is no green monkey in Africa running around biting people and giving them AIDS, but there is a real-life mad White power structure creating and using deadly viruses.

African/African American women must look the monster in its eyes. African people the world over are being used as worthless guinea pigs while simultaneously being destroyed in huge numbers. The African/African American woman's quest to reduce the spread of AIDS is directly related to the necessity of stopping patriarchal White supremacy. White supremacy is the *true* disease; AIDS is only another deadly symptom of pathological White supremacy. AIDS is designed to rid the White supremacists of their genetically dominant enemies. So, while it is necessary to get all African people to practice abstinence, safe sex, and to stop drug usage, a major thrust must be the undoing of the White supremacist value/behavior system that is simply hell-bent on getting rid of all African people.

CHAPTER 5

WHITE MALE SUPREMACY

"Yurugu, originally named Ogo, is described in Dogon mythology as acting with "anxiety and impatience." He is "incessantly restless," in search of the secrets of Amma (the creative principle), of which he wants to "gain possession." He is known for his aggressiveness and incompleteness. He is in a state of solitude, having been deprived of his female principle; he is also impotent. When Yurugu, "the pale fox," reaches his final form of development, he is "the permanent element of disorder in the universe," the "agent of disorganization." He was "marked" from birth for failure, to remain forever incomplete; to search perpetually for his female principle. He is not only the agent of cosmic disorder, but also of psychological individualization."

Marimba Ani in *Yurugu: An African-Centered Critique of European Cultural Thought and Behavior*

"...and be on the lookout for those spirit snipers, trying to steal your life..."

Public Enemy's *He Got Game*

It must first be understood and eagerly accepted that women—Native American, African, and nonwhite—must be equally involved in the battle to end White supremacy. Women are often victims three times over, and it would be unwise to not take a vital part in their own liberation. After all, when women are liberated, entire

25

families, communities, and nations are simultaneously liberated. And when women are oppressed, their families, communities, and nations are also oppressed. Either women must be included or take over the liberation quest. bell hooks, in her book *Killing Rage: Ending Racism*, states:

> When race and racism are the topic in public discourse the voices that speak are male. There is no large body of social and political critique by women on the topics of race and racism.[1]

Nonwhite men cannot end patriarchal White male supremacy without women. It would be foolish and unwise to even try. If fighting White supremacy remains a "men only" task, then we're all doomed! bell hooks states:

> Not listening to the voices of progressive black women means that black political discourse on race always suffers from critical gaps in theoretical vision and concrete strategy.[2]

We cannot afford to look in the mirror and realize that the battle against patriarchal White supremacy was lost because we were the enemy. Women *must* be a leading and supporting element. Men of color must realize that they simultaneously sabotage their struggle for liberation and oppress women when they attempt to exclude them from an active role in the liberation of their people.

Insecurity, fear, self-doubt—these negative emotional-psychological states fuel the engine of patriarchal White male supremacy. As a group, White men have formed a fraternity of whiteness whose agenda is to eliminate their collective feelings of insecurity, fear, and self-doubt that have plagued them for centuries. Their paranoid, immoral, violent rulership has but one goal: Keep White men safe. Safe from what? Genetic annihilation.

> The Color-Confrontation theory states that the white or color-deficient Europeans responded psychologically, with a profound sense of numerical inadequacy and color inferiority, in their confrontations with the majority of the world's people—all of whom possessed varying degrees of color-producing capacity. This psychological response, whether conscious or unconscious, revealed an inadequacy based on the most obvious and fundamental part of their being, their external appearance. As might be anticipated. . . whites defensively developed an uncontrollable sense of hostility and aggression.[3]

The fears, insecurities, and self-doubt of the White male collective, along with their subtle and not-so-subtle defense mechanisms, are imbued into every facet of White rule making and enforcement. White businessmen and politicians agree that *White men must remain on top by any means necessary.* Any means justifies this end. Laws, policies, and rules change according to their needs and concerns. Unfairness and perversion (which the public is missocialized to view as normal) become the order of the day. This is a much worse scenario than inmates running the asylum.

Now, what is the White man's relationship to White women? Not *with* White women, but *to* White women. Fearful, insecure, and self-doubting White men do not have relationships with their women or anyone else except the White male members in their fraternity of whiteness. They do, however, relate *to* others in various ways. Relating to people instead of relating *with* people creates an "us" versus "them" interaction. To keep themselves on top, they must believe that differences equal deficiencies. Insecure White males believe that they could not survive without this system. This is the social system in which Americans and most Westerners are reared. In such a spiritually and morally void social system, people are taught to spend their lives proving that they are superior to others. This quest for superiority gives rise to an intense, self-destructive pattern of behavior which dysfunctionalizes human relationships. The natural order of human nature is converted to disorder. The fearful, insecure, self-doubting White male needs and feeds off this disorder.

For the most part, relationships and marriages formed under White supremacy have been made in hell. Fearful, insecure, self-doubting rulers create a personal-worth-ranking mentality and a better-than-thou competitiveness into the values of the population under their rule. Lustful so-called relationships, financial debt, spouse abuse, domestic violence, and high divorce rates are to be expected under such a destructive value system. The fact that many White men suffer because of patriarchal White male supremacy is accepted by their fraternity; White casualties are expected and accepted. Paranoid, angry, ruthless, fearful: These are the characteristics of the White male power structure. Question: What are the sexual habits of such men, and how have their habits influenced other women and men?

Contrary to media opinion, our parents did not teach us about love and sex. It is from the sexually insecure, frustrated, and perverted White male power structure that we learn about love and sex.

Rape was also an acceptable, albeit unofficially stated, behavior exhibited by White males, especially towards nonwhite women. According to Angela Y. Davis, rape of African women during the European slave trade was manifested in an "institutionalized pattern."[4] Ms. Davis goes on to state:

> It would be a mistake to regard the institutionalized pattern of rape during slavery as an expression of white men's sexual urges, otherwise stifled by the specter of white womanhood's chastity. That would be far too simplistic an explanation. Rape was a weapon of domination, a weapon of repression, whose covert goal was to extinguish slave women's will to resist, and in the process, to demoralize their men.[5]

Thus, patriarchal White supremacy has always used sexual weaponry as a means of dehumanizing women. Rape assaults the very essence of the female self. And it is this destruction of women's sense of self that gives feelings of power in the White male power structure.

As a result of the social conditioning instilled in us by a system controlled by such men, women, men, and even children are better at performing various sexual acts than they are at developing and maintaining the psychological and spiritual elements of love. Lustfulness to the point of perversion is the order of the day. Women catch much hell because men expect sex first and love later—if at all. Any and everything that are right and productive are now topsy-turvy. A truly sad and pathetic element of this pathology is the African male who has, through social conditioning and miseducation, taken on the abusive, perverted behavior of White men toward their African sisters.

One should not be surprised by the various sexual perversions coming out of White male supremacist rulership. Child pornography, for example, can flourish in nations such as America because EVERY human being is programmed to be a sex oriented consumer who eventually becomes a sexualized object. This includes children. Under the White male power structure, the innocence of childhood gives way to sexy little kids. This is what has given rise to a multimillion dollar child pornography industry. These children are, in truth, killed before having a chance to grow. Pornography is essentially pimping, raping, and exploiting women under the euphemisms of "free will" and "free enterprise." African American men have once again taken up the harmful habits of White men by establishing their own pornography businesses which exploit African American women. African American women and children (female and male children) are placed in the flesh for sale ads by both White and African American men.

Sex, under White male supremacy, is brutish, lustful, and mean-spirited. Sex becomes a war in which women are conquered by men. Conquerors have the right to reward or punish the conquered as they see fit, which is why it is important to have "sexual conquests." All of these beliefs and practices stem from the feelings of insecurity and paranoia that are inherent in the patriarchal White male power structure. Women often spend many years trying not to be conquered by men. Women are equal and must continue to demand to be treated as equals.

"Conquered" women often become victims of sexual violence. It has always been permissible to abuse conquered, subjugated people, especially women. The pathology of the White male power structure is vividly manifested in its conditioning and programming of the population to be insensitive to women's feelings, views, and overall condition.

In his book on serial killers (*Signature Killers*), Robert D. Keppel discusses the impact of pornography:

> However, I do believe that repetitive violence, especially violence perpetrated on women, has a cumulative effect that desensitizes a viewer over time to what should be an abhorrence of violence. If it's now formulaic to terrorize women, because we see it in every movie of the week...and off and on in various series, the pattern of perpetrating that terror goes into a common culture...It's one thing to be stimulated by beautiful women and romance, but it's quite another to be handed a video manual for how to kidnap, beat up, rape, assault, murder, and humiliate a woman...much television and movie programming contains what amounts to little more than a stereotyping guide for how to handle women who are too aggressive, promiscuous, pushy, contrary, and however else women can be categorized.[6]

In America the saying is "boys will be boys." So, when boys/men abuse girls/women, they're simply being themselves. Such behavior is expected of them. The White male power structure cannot and will not foster humane, kind, spiritual values designed to develop healthy female-male relationships. Miseducated men and conquered women will not see eye-to-eye because they've been socially conditioned to self-destruct.

Under White male supremacy, it is common to hear men describe their sexual relations with women as if describing a boxing match, football game, or a battle. Some men enjoy describing how they bring tears to women's eyes during sex because of the pain they inflicted in her vagina or anus. Many men have convinced themselves that women are masochistic. Young boys are socially conditioned to "sow their oats" in females; this means that males are *SUPPOSED* to sexually mistreat/abuse females.

So, what type of sexual norms is developed under the paranoid, angry, ruthless White male supremacist power structure? Perverted sex; sex as conquest/violence; sex as competition; sex as sport; sex as a way to mask insecurities—all of these and nothing else. In his book, *The IceMan Inheritance: Prehistoric Sources of Western Man's Racism, Sexism and Aggression*, Michael Bradley explains that hundreds of thousands of years living in ice-age Europe not only contributed to the aggressive nature of Europeans, but also to sexual inadequacies which leads to sexual frustrations and various forms of sexual perversions, including sexual violence.[7]

Understand: Women are exploited by a patriarchal power structure that feels totally comfortable in using violence against women; hence, *women are supposed to be mistreated!*

Such is the nature of the madness under which millions of women exist, struggling to truly live. How will this pathological condition end? The answer lies not only in the hands of men, but equally in the hands of oppressed women.

CHAPTER 6

THE MYTH OF WHITE NORMALCY

"...the white color of the skin is not natural to man, but that by nature he has a black or brown skin, like our fore-fathers the Hindus;...a white man has never originally sprung from the womb of nature..."
                                        Arthur Schopenhauer

"The white race is the cancer of history. It is the white race and it alone--its ideologies and inventions---which eradicates autonomous civilizations wherever it spreads, which has upset the ecological balance of the planet, which now threatens the very existence of life itself."
                                        Susan Sontag

White folk is a miracle of affliction.
                    Alice Walker's *The Color Purple*

More than 200 years of White supremacist teach-ings, via education, religion, media, and government and corporate policies, of *different* (meaning nonwhite) equals *inferior* (meaning people of color, especially Africans), have made many of the earth's people believe that the val-ues, teachings, and behavior of Caucasian people are the standards for all humans. People of color close their eyes, open their mouths, and swallow whatever amount of miseducation is placed in their minds by institutions (edu-cational, religious, etc.) controlled and operated by the White male power structure. As Samuel Clemens said "...a truth is not hard to kill and a lie told well is immortal."[1]

Deceit and hypocrisy are inherent in the values, cul-ture, and psychology of White culture.[2] Marimba Ani's statement that "Within the nature of European culture there

33

exists a statement of value or of "moral" behavior that has no meaning for the members of that culture"[3] reeks of what Bobby Wright called a psychopathic racial personality.[4] This means that women (including White women) and people of color are dealing with an extremely dangerous personality and power structure. As for White women, they must, again, examine their thoughts and feelings around their Whiteness, especially as this relates to participating in a liberation struggle with their Sisters of color. Marimba Ani, in chapter 6 of her book *Yurugu*, mentioned that Europeans want to appear as caring or "ideal" people, especially to non-Europeans, because this allows Europeans to manipulate and exploit non-Europeans.[5] Marimba Ani states:

> It is an inherent characteristic of the culture that it prepares members of the culture to be able to act like friends toward those they regard as enemies; to be able to convince others that they have come to help when they, in fact, have come to destroy the others and their culture. That some may "believe" that they are actually doing good only makes them more dangerous, for they have swallowed their own rhetoric--perhaps a convenient self-delusion. Hypocritical behavior is sanctioned and rewarded in European culture.[6]

Hence, women are fighting a dishonest, treacherous White supremacist patriarchal power structure that is hell bent on keeping its power. Oppressed populations under its control are conditioned to contribute to their own oppression by way of programmed immorality-based thinking and behavior. The victims are too busy conning one another to comprehend the true reality. Marimba Ani states, "European culture is constructed in such a way that successful survival within it discourages honesty and directness and encourages dishonesty and deceit..."[7] Women must beware of how they handle conflicting beliefs, how they deal with varying attitudes, differing so-cial-economic status, and racial differences. Being for the struggle is the most significant factor. Women must not allow themselves to get caught in a spiral of confusion that will only serve to maintain their oppression.

The myth of White normalcy began in the 15th century with the European conquest, enslavement, and colonization of the world.[8] As historian John Henrik Clarke has often stated, Europeans not only colonized the world, they also colonized information about the world. White intellectuals and scholars viewed nonwhite peoples and their cultures as barbaric, heathen, and uncivilized. Black, brown, red, and yellow people from Africa, Asia, North America, South America, Australia, and the Pacific Isle nations were viewed as inferior savages that needed the civilizing attributes of White people.[9] Every aspect of what we call education has come from the minds of White men and women who view nonwhites as *different*. In the minds of the White power structure, different means inferior to Whites.

After centuries of Caucasian domination of the planet and the ensuing miseducation, many nonwhite people began viewing themselves as inferior who could only become worthy through Caucasian approval. Non-whites, therefore, began to unquestioningly believe in and imitate Caucasians. In a degrading, almost childlike fashion, people of color the world over spend most or all of their lives mimicking what may be the most pathological people on earth.

Cold. Collectively speaking, the very nature of Caucasians is cold. This coldness manifests itself in the violent, insensitive, and immoral manner in which Caucasians have encountered other nations for the past 500 years. The story is more known today than it was just several years ago—murder, slavery, the deliberate spreading of disease, rape of people and earth, and the evil use of religion. Of all the racial groups, the White race should be the last to be held up as the model of human dignity and accomplishment. In all earnestness, the collective behavior of the White race has been and remains pathological. It is both unfortunate and scary that much of the nonwhite world has been, and still remains the imitators of madness.

The clever, evil mixture of laws, religion, marketing, military might, and skin color is the staple of White supremacist madness. We feel totally free while in fact we are all slaves of pathological beliefs which we believe are normal. In America, we believe that we smoke cigarettes, drink intoxicating beverages, eat junk foods, drive fast, and watch countless hours of mind destroying television because we *want to*. We agree with same-sex marriages because we *want to*. We throw elderly people into nursing homes because we *want to*. We actually believe that our beliefs and values are *our* beliefs and values. The molders of our value system delight in the fact that they can implant self-destructive beliefs and not be found out. They literally cast stones and successfully hide their hands.

Women, even White women, must critically examine the myth of White normalcy if they are to obtain self-determination. There is no self-determination in the shadow of White madness. Perhaps the greatest harm, besides instilling self-hate, is nonwhites' total dependency on White people. Unfortunately, the question for many people of color is, "How can I survive without having White approval?" The mental and spiritual death which accompanies White imitation goes unnoticed. The price of freedom demands that we break away from the myth of the White normal. Marimba Ani states, "A friend of mine points out that Europeans would indeed destroy each other if they did not have "others" to destroy."[10] People of color are in the psychopath's category of the "other." This realization should give women no illusions as to what they are fighting against.

CHAPTER 7

AFRICAN AMERICAN MEN:
INNOCENT OR GUILTY?

African American men must stand trial. We must be judged. Do we knowingly and willingly participate in oppressing and abusing African American women? Do we ignore or condone the abuse of African American women by other Brothers and White men? The innocence or guilt of African American men lies in the perceptions of African American women. They are best qualified to evaluate our behavior.

As with African Americans in general, African American men are somewhat of a Frankenstein creation. Frankenstein was created not by God but by a man, an arrogant man who wanted to become God. Frankenstein was not created to be a self-determining creation, but a programmed creation. From the cradle to the grave, African American men are made into Frankensteins via the images, behaviors, and philosophies of White men. These are promoted as the standards of normality. Think about it: White men called us niggers, and we adopted the habit (and sometimes proudly) of referring to ourselves as niggers. White men called our women bitches, and we adopted the habit of proudly calling our women bitches. White men physically beat their women, and we followed suit, beating our women. Almost all African American women who are physically brutalized are done so by African American, not White, men. We conked, gerri curled, and permed our hair so that we could resemble White men. Before the Western slave trade, Africans did not call themselves "nigger." We did not refer to African women as "bitches," nor did we physically abuse them. Such madness was not even a remote possibility in our native culture. But after more than 250 years of being Americanized, we have lost our minds, and many African American men have lost self-respect and respect for others.

The heart breaking reality is that some African American males, from elementary age to the elderly, believe that it's okay to degrade African American females. Whether they are Brothers with doctorate degrees or high school dropouts, too many of us refer to our Sisters as "fine bitches," "freaks," and "hoes" without giving it a second thought. We encourage the Black woman to physically degrade her body by engaging in pornography. Ironically, as soon as someone calls our sister or mother one of these degrading names we want to blow his brains out! This tells me that deep inside we know it's wrong to degrade the African woman, but old habits die hard. And since the entire world gets to see (hear) African American men degrade African American women on comedy shows, movies, and some rap songs, is it any wonder that the White power structure routinely abuses African American women and that many Sisters don't believe that the Black men have their backs?

Apathetic, ignorant, and miseducated African American men cannot protect women. And since it is considered "manly" to sexually exploit and degrade women, it becomes increasingly frightening to visualize the future of the African American community. On one end there's the adolescent African American male who uses the words "bitch" and "hoe" with tremendous pride, and on the other there's the professional African American adult male who relishes his playboy lifestyle. Both find delight in deceiving and exploiting African American women. Neither benefits their people, especially African American women.

Since no African American male comes out of his mother's womb with degrading thoughts about females, it is necessary that conscious Brothers and Sisters confront African American men and boys on their degrading treatment of females by developing rites of passage programs in African American communities that are designed to teach manhood skills. Some of us believe that the rites of passage idea is too idealistic; but it is necessary. In many Eastern societies, adolescence has a definite ending and adulthood has a definite beginning, both of which are celebrated by rites of passage. As a result, most Eastern societies do not experience the degree of madness that is so prevalent in the United States. In America, however, there is no clear cut-off age for adolescence, and this is a large part of the problem facing African Americans. We have 17-year-olds acting like Al Pacino's character Tony Montana in the movie *Scarface*. We have 19 year-olds acting like Wesley Snipes' character Nino Brown in *New Jack City*. We have 25-year-olds acting like Martin Lawrence's buffoonish characters in his sit-com and movies. We have 50-year-old men hanging in night clubs trying to seduce women. Chris Rock said you never want to be the old guy at the club. Probably more than any other group in America, Africans need community-based rites of passage programs for our boys and girls.

We have too many hot boys, bad boys, toy boys, and play boys, but not enough *MEN*. African American women must give strong messages to African American men that no miseducated, apathetic, confused, disrespectful boys, regardless of age, will be allowed into their lives. The Sisters must tell their daughters and one another to not speak to anyone who says to them, "Pssst, yo' shorty, let me holla at ya." African American women must refuse to date any man who can find nothing more interesting about them than their pretty face, fine legs, breasts, hips, and other body parts. The madness is perpetuated whenever women decide to engage in such superficial relationships with men. There is a saying that steel sharpens steel and men sharpen men, but under white male supremacy, conscious African American women must take the lead in demanding that African American males straighten up. Men will change when women demand nothing less than a change for the better. The American power structure will never develop conscious, committed, competent African American men. It prefers to have miseducated, immature, disrespectful, apathetic African American males. Women can deal a powerful blow to the system by refusing to compromise themselves with **males** and by dealing only with **men**.

Some African American men, if asked about their innocence or guilt, would say that they don't do anything that women don't allow them to do. Such Brothers are simply justifying their treacherous ways. Even if a woman allows herself to be exploited to get or keep a man, this is still no justification for the man to exploit her. He is still wrong because, as an African man, he has the responsibility of protecting his woman, and he cannot protect her and abuse her at the same time.

African American women must also check their own beliefs and behaviors, such as dating several men at once, wearing extremely revealing clothes in public, and putting up with the lame excuses some Brothers give for dogging Sisters. Understand: If a man believes that women are whores, he's going to treat women like whores. Faced with such sick thinking among some African American men, the African American woman must socially and psychologically educate Black men. It is unfortunate that this burden, along with many others, must be placed on the shoulders of African American women. But women must set the standard for Black manhood, and that standard must lead to more Brothers becoming committed fathers, husbands, and community leaders.

So, are African American men innocent or guilty of assisting in the oppression of African American women? Not all African American women will agree and views are likely to be mixed, but we all agree that some African American men need help, and it is my belief that the kind of help the Brothers need can most effectively come from the demands and standards set by African American women. Yes, steel sharpens steel and men may sharpen men, but as sojourners in the hells of North America, African American men need the steel that only African American women possess. I believe women are up to the challenge. You are the mother of creation. You are the first teachers of our children. Men may think they are stronger based on bench pressing, but real strength is measured by staying with your children, working on your marriage, and avoiding suicide.

CHAPTER 8

PATRIARCHY AND FEMALE SUBJUGATION

Patriarchy is a cultural philosophy and practice that originated with European men. It is indeed unfortunate for women of color that their oppressed men would take up the blood-stained blade of patriarchy and use it against women. bell hooks discusses this madness in her book *Killing Rage: Ending Racism.*[1] I absolutely agree with bell hooks' statement that women should not feel less feminine because they choose to speak against racism.[2] Patriarchy basically espouses the belief that it is impossible, by nature, for women to be equal to men. Women leave their mothers' wombs inferior to men. Thus, female subjugation becomes the natural order of things. Patriarchy's practice of a family's lineage being based on the father is not the natural order of things. African civilizations, which are the oldest known to humankind, were matriarchal.[3] Africans had no problem worshiping goddesses, such as Hathor and Asset (Isis), or having female rulers, such as Queen Candace, Queen Nzingha, and Nefertiti, to name a few.

Although the paranoid, insecure patriarchal White male power structure allows some White females to hold oppressorship positions, it is intimidated by the presence of a female sense of self. Under White male supremacy, a female is encouraged to become a woman only when she conforms to the boundaries forced upon her. Women can be subjugated only if they, through missocialization or fear, consent to being subjugated. Those whom White supremacy subjugates, White supremacy destroys; this is the ultimate danger of patriarchy. In ways both subtle and obvious, it is okay to exploit, physically beat, deceive, terrorize and, yes, kill women—especially nonwhite and poor women.

How is it that a woman is good enough to have life come through her body but not good enough to have lineage passed through her? For thousands of years and even to this day, the Africans had no problem with this.

> The matriarchal system is the base of the social organization in Egypt and throughout Black Africa. In contrast, there has never been any proof of the existence of a paleo-Mediterranean matriarchy, supposedly exclusively white.[4]

So, what's wrong with the White male power structure? They can't comprehend *equality*. White male logic cannot conceive of a man and woman standing on equal footing. They can't see the complementary nature of man and woman because their warped system is based on fear of differences, competition, and violence. Thus, matriarchy is synonymous with weakness. It is clear that very little woman-man harmony can exist under such a system.

> The matriarchal system proper is characterized by the collaboration and harmonious flowering of both sexes, and by a certain preeminence of woman in society, due originally to economic conditions, but accepted and even defended by man.[5]

The above quote states a reality that was and is widely believed by African people. One cannot help but wonder if the Black man's historical worship of and respect for the Black woman generates a certain fear in the

White male power structure. Whether this pathological fear is psychosexually based or stems from the fear of genetic annihilation (as relates to people of color), the fact remains that White males in power *fear* feeling inferior to women. This fear could be the foundation upon which patriarchy rests. The modern Western culture of macho, muscled manliness is a mask that hides the White male's fear of womanhood. African and other nonwhite men have been miseducated into believing that all men have this fear of women and equality with women. They don't realize that their salvation lies in being on equal footing with women. A man and woman that enjoy mutual respect for one another are better able to combat patriarchal White male supremacy. The lie that men and women are in competition with one another is an effective divide-and-conquer strategy of the White male power structure.

Patriarchy is instilled in young boys through a socialization process that allows boys to conduct themselves inappropriately: "boys will be boys" or "he's only sowing his oats" or "he really likes the ladies." Patriarchy condones and, to a large extent, encourages male misbehavior. The underlying patriarchal message in this childhood socialization process is "males are more valued than females." This sets the stage. Male socialization under patriarchal White male supremacy makes it virtually impossible for men to form nonsuperficial relationships with women. Na'im Akbar says that adult men are kept at "the boy stage" of development, and girls become their toys. A popular Western saying is, "Boys will have their toys."

Patriarchy also teaches women to never, under any circumstances, question male authority. This "father knows best" aspect of the patriarchal system ignores, frustrates, and suppresses female mindpower and pays no attention to the wealth of experiences women have to share. This practice, while beneficial to the patriarchal White male power structure, is absolutely destructive to women and oppressed men. For example, the African American woman and man should perceive themselves as one body fighting an unjust White supremacist system, but they don't. Women are seldom invited to voice their opinions or share information and, as a result our families, institutions, and communities are not balanced. Allowed to continue we will perish. White supremacy takes beliefs and practices that are good for its survival, and teaches its victims that these same beliefs and practices are also good for them. This diabolical scheme is very effective.

Any belief and practice that teach or force women to not question men is divisive and dysfunctional. It is ridiculous and impossible to even imagine that men have all the answers. This serves to reveal another facet within the pathological nature of the patriarchal White male supremacist power structure: pathology is healthy and dysfunctionality is functional. The victims of White male supremacy often see right as wrong and upside down as rightside up.

Patriarchal practice and philosophy are a frontal assault on women, healthy female-male relationships, and common sense. The fears and insecurities of the White male power structure needs patriarchy in order for them to feel in control of themselves and everyone else.

CHAPTER 9

CREATING THE DYSFUNCTIONAL MOTHER

Damned if you do
Damned if you don't.
                              Author unknown

The "crazy" or dysfunctional woman is primarily
the creation of insecure White male power holders. To
really understand certain definitions and terms, it is necessary to examine the mentality of those who created them.
Since America was established on the beliefs, opinions,
fears, and desires of Anglo-Saxon/English/White men,
every behavior exhibited by nonwhites and females is sub-
ject to ridicule, oppression, or elimination. White men
possess a collective brotherhood-of-rulership mentality that
is in full operation even when they are at war. The creation and maintenance of power (which White men define
as the ability to dominate and destroy others) absolutely
require that the White male ruler dysfunctionalizes any
thought or behavior that does not arise from his own mind.
Mothers, especially nonwhite and poor, are the daily tar-
gets of such madness.

The mentality existing among the collective White
male psyche contains a weird schizophrenic psychopathol-
ogy that upholds the sanctity of family while implementing
racist and sexist policies that prevent people from forming and supporting healthy families. The economic reality of American society discourages many men and women
from getting married and starting families. Some people
will marry but not produce children because of the cost of
rearing them. Let's examine how misdefining manhood

negatively impacts womanhood. America defines manhood as a male with large sums of money. In this sick definition of manhood, a millionaire is superior to a man earning $7 an hour. The psychological impact of this definition is nothing less than devastating. Many men accept it as true and, unfortunately, so do many women.

The values that truly make a man are ignored, to the detriment of all—especially women. America has become a nation of hypnotized carrot chasers that are too busy and too miseducated to ask the question, "Whose principles govern my thoughts and actions?" Women cannot reach their true potential until they understand and help eradicate this definition of manhood that is solely based on large sums of money. The men who believe this deliberately misdefined definition of manhood will most likely treat women like "things" instead of human beings. The women who believe this sick definition of manhood tend to unconsciously live their lives as if they are on an auction block, ready to be purchased by the man with the largest salary. Women are dysfunctionalized through the dysfunctionalizing of men. Under such a social structure, men and women become predator and prey.

If a mother is dysfunctional, it is because White male power holders view "good" as that which makes money and "bad" as that which does not make money. Coupling this with the practice of defining humans along racial, gender, and economic lines, one can see that the patriarchal White male power structure is the largest perpetrator of human destruction.

Men are not qualified to define womanhood. Although many men have, at various points throughout history, exploited women, White men, collectively speaking, act as if they carried women in their wombs and gave birth to women. The arrogance of White male power has launched a frontal assault on Mother Nature herself. Such a suicidal assault on nature should give a very clear signal to women. They must free their minds and souls from the hell of White male domination.

Miseducation and self-destructive definitions of manhood and womanhood have programmed many women to believe in the many psychiatric labels of emotional and mental disturbance. Many women run to male therapists, expecting to be rescued from the storms of life. Women must come together and discuss the origin of the pressures they face. Women must understand that psychiatric labels project onto victims the insecurities and disfunctions of white males. In fact, many of the disturbances women suffer are a natural and perfectly understandable reaction to oppression.

CHAPTER 10

HOW PUBLIC SCHOOLS PRESENT MOTHERS
AS PERPETRATORS

Patriarchal White male dominated American society has committed an almost unforgivable injustice to single mothers, poor mothers, and nonwhite mothers with school-age children. Mothers are often blamed for the ills plaguing American schools. "Their mothers don't care" and similar statements are frequently made by some teachers, principals, school board members, politicians, social service workers, and policemen. These so-called professionals find scapegoating easier than examining the causative factors that will expose the true perpetrators. Blaming the victim is easy when the victim is a woman—especially if she is nonwhite, poor, and single. Who really speaks for these women?

Scapegoating mothers as perpetrators is a very effective smokescreen designed to prevent society from searching for causes. When the public examines causes, the political-corporate White male power structure begins to sweat. The patriarchal power structure keeps the public ignorant through miseducation. This ignorance is dangerous because blaming victims creates more victims. The cause of economic and psychological stress (patriarchal White male power structure) goes unaddressed. Every day another nonwhite, poor, or single mother is unfairly labeled a perpetrator. Sadly, some of these mothers, after hearing and reading the negative views of them, come to believe that they are not good mothers—that they are dysfunctional. Many of them do not understand the factors that led to their oppressed, depressed condition. The true perpetrators, however, understand.

The children of victimized mothers are targeted, labeled, and oppressed at school. What should be an environment for growth becomes an environment of stagnation and destruction. Teachers and principals who view these children's mothers as dysfunctional tends to treat the children like patients instead of students. In my book, *Kill Them Before They Grow: Misdiagnosis of African American Boys in American Classrooms*, I discussed how these children are often miseducated, labeled, diagnosed, placed in special education or inferior classes, and medicated. All of this is done for the school's convenience, not to help the children. Is it any wonder that many of these children develop negative attitudes toward school? A child can sense the hatred coming from teachers and principals. Imagine the frustration these children feel— knowing something is wrong but not being able to articulate this to someone! They eventually bond with other victims and rebel in various ways. Their rebellion against educational oppression causes both child and mother to be oppressed even more by the system.

Just as many rape victims are blamed for their rape, nonwhite, poor, or single mothers are blamed and punished for being nonwhite, poor, or single. The fact that many of these mothers are excellent parents is deliberately ignored. A patriarchal White male controlled system that spends its time and resources condemning mothers is a system in decline. And, as I'm sure you've heard, as the family goes so goes the nation.

The children of oppressed mothers are oppressed across the board. In some American cities, teen curfews designed to keep children and teens off the streets past a certain time have been established. In some cities, parents are locked up if their children violate curfew. Although a mother may be at work, believing her child to be at home or school, she will be picked up from her job by police or subpoenaed; in either case, she will be fined by a juvenile court judge. This pathetic practice exploits and criminalizes entire families. Many of these exploited mothers do not know that some of the policies and practices that abuse them were created by elected officials who received their votes. Dealing with politics will be discussed under the recommendations section of this book.

Every woman must take the intellectual and moral challenge of freeing their minds of the miseducational social-political-economic teachings of the patriarchal White male power structure, and then see the diabolical truth about the abuse and oppression of many mothers in America and the world. Upon examination, many will find that the line separating them from middle-class or victim-mother is very thin. Given an unfortunate experience, such as job loss, one can easily become a victim-mother. The White male power structure knows this, but others that point accusatory fingers at these mothers do not understand that they, too, can easily become victims.

The true perpetrator, the patriarchal White male power structure, uses every institution under its domain to confuse, divide, conquer, and rule women and oppressed nonwhite and poor men. If an institution such as the public school system doesn't work for the victims, this is because it is working extremely well for the White male rulers. In their struggle for true self-determination, women must not become confused by the logic of the patriarchal White male power structure. Up may be down and down may be up. The standard operating procedures of agencies and institutions under patriarchal White male control *must* function in an unfair and frustrating manner in order to keep the victims confused and divided.

PART TWO

THE WOMEN

CHAPTER 1

AFRICAN AMERICAN WOMEN:
THE CRUCIFIXION OF MOTHER

"Assailed on the one hand by white patriarchy and on the other hand by sexist black men and racist white women, black women must be ever vigilant in our struggle to challenge and transform the devaluation of black womanhood."

bell hooks' Killing Rage: Ending Racism

The more blackness a woman has, the more beautiful she is.

Alex Haley's Roots

Mother was present before the creation of the earth. Mother was there when God said, "Let Us make man." Mother was happy to assist. Mother decorated the earth and assisted in the naming and placing of its creatures and the sun-kissed people. In her sacred ebony nakedness, Mother bathed in the refreshing waters of the earth's oceans, seas, rivers, and lakes. She ate luscious fruit as They walked hand-in-hand across the earth, marveling at Their work. They are the Original Family; the givers of life. <u>Who could dare hate and abuse such a mother!?</u>

Mother was traded, like a trinket, by those who have been consumed by the Prince of Evil. Dragged through the thicket, Mother was bound and placed in the holes of ships to be delivered to worshippers of Satan. She was auctioned to demons while Her sisters were kept at home to be colonized by madmen.

Repeatedly bought, sold, and raped, Mother shed tears that carried messages to God saying, "Please don't let Your heart be broken over what they do to Me. They are merely ignorant adolescents possessed by evil; give them time to redeem themselves." Mother is merciful and patient.

Mother scrubbed floors in the houses of the arrogantly ignorant whose sources of wealth were manifested by their blood-stained hands. It was Mother's mahogany colored breasts which were suckled by those who would inherit the wealth of their fathers.

Mother's heart broke many times as the earth's original men hung from trees; their necks stretched as their lifeless bodies were smiled upon by happy murderers. Mother wondered if they would ever be able to redeem themselves.

Mother. She who has walked in spirit and flesh for unfathomed millenniums; She was with God when God said to Her, "Let Us make man." She who adorned the universe with the smiles of babies, and named them "stars." She, through whose womb we entered this world. Mother. How dare they disrespect, batter, and exploit Her! Through their Satanic lifestyle, the arrogant evil has crucified Mother. Can they redeem themselves?

In America's past as in its present, the reality of African American women is a reality of oppression by design. Psychological mutilation, the violence of rape and forced breeding, rearing the oppressor's children, and performing menial and degrading work constitutes the foundation laid for African American women. This Black woman, the original mother on planet earth, continues to endure attacks on the very legitimacy of her existence. From the cradle to the grave, this original mother is confronted and attacked by the Anglo-Saxon images of Barbie, Cinderella, Snow White, and a host of other Caucasian images of beauty. Her full figure, full lips, broad nose, tightly curled hair, and dark skin were purposely presented as abnormal by the White controlled print and electronic media. In her book *Black Looks: Race and Representation*, bell hooks states:

> If we compare the relative progress African Americans have made in education and employment to the struggle to gain control over how we are represented, particularly in the mass media, we see that there has been little change in the area of representation. Opening a magazine or book, turning on the television set, watching a film, or looking at photographs in public spaces, we are most likely to see images of black people that reinforce and reinscribe white supremacy.[1]

The African woman went from being the earth's first goddess to patriarchal White male supremacy's exploited and raped worker. She has been the worker of the world. Angela Y. Davis, in *Women Race & Class*, states:

> Proportionately, more Black women have always worked outside their homes than have their white sisters. The enormous space that work occupies in Black women's lives today follows a pattern established during the very earliest days of slavery. As slaves, compulsory labor over-shadowed every other aspect of women's existence...the starting point for any exploration of Black women's lives under slavery would be an appraisal of their role as workers.[2]

White male dominated governmental-corporate entities have, since the abolition of the European slave trade, targeted African American women to become the lifeblood of its social service agencies, many of its businesses (as consumers only), and its prisons (which are really neoslave plantations). Approximately half of all African American households are headed by the mother, with more than 1.2 million African American women in the fast growing ranks of the working poor.[3] This harsh reality is one reason that African American families constitute 39 percent of families on welfare.[4] The almost slave-like condition of too many African American women is what forces them into system-maintaining social service agencies that often treat them like cattle (see part 3: Social Welfare and Women). Their men? The condition of African American men, as you know, is deplorable—more than 1.5 million in prison, high homicide rates, suicide, AIDS, underemployment, unemployment. This genocidal double-whammy can confuse and frustrate African American women, but they must not allow themselves to be overwhelmed. She must be calm, level-headed, and strategic in overcoming the madness of White male supremacy.

The African American woman is the one whose hair is "too short." She's the one whose hips are "too big." This original woman is the one mostly labeled "welfare queen" and "unfit mother." The racist double standards and policies of patriarchal White male America are designed to instill self-hate, self-blame, and frustration into the African American woman in order to weaken her. She carries a cross that is three times her size. Even some of her own men, due to White supremacist miseducation, victimize her—if not physical victimization, then by condemning her for not being Snow White, Cinderella, or Barbie.

One of the best methods of dividing, conquering, and oppressing a people is to condition them to view one another in a negative manner. This strategy, for the most part, is used effectively on African Americans. It is not uncommon to hear some African American children, women, and men describe one another as having "good hair" or "bad hair." Some African Americans believe that only very fair complexioned African Americans are attractive. Many dark complexioned African American women are especially subjected to such demoralizing scrutiny. The energy of oppressed people must be used to end their oppression; not one scintilla of their energy should go to fighting one another. The African American woman has had more than two centuries—and counting—of being programmed for self-ridicule and self-hate. Her task is no easy one. While fighting White male supremacy, she must simultaneously reeducate some of her own people. The attainment of self-determination, however, is well worth the struggle. bell hooks states:

> Their little girl is just reaching that stage of preadolescent life where we become obsessed with our image, with how we look and how others see us. Her skin is dark. Her hair chemically straightened. Not only is she fundamentally convinced that straightened hair is more beautiful than curly, kinky, natural hair, she believes that lighter skin makes one more valuable in the eyes of others. Despite her parents' effort to raise their children in an affirming black context, she has internalized white supremacist values and aesthetics, a way of looking and seeing the world that negates her value.[5]

Today, the African American woman is being tracked into America's prison plantations along with her man. She, too, is being robbed of the most productive years of her life, and her children are being robbed of their mother. The sanctity of her womanhood and her family deliberately goes unacknowledged by the White male supremacist system. The system counts on single African American women eventually needing some kind of assistance and struggling to provide for household necessities. Many will become slaves to their debtors. Her oppressive condition brings pleasure to the sadistic White male rulers, many of whom, ironically, desire and seek sexual intimacy with her.

Betrayed by White female headed liberation movements, and seeing only White women reap the rewards of the civil rights movement, the African American woman has come to understand that Sisters must unite and develop political agendas designed to empower African American communities. This need is evidenced by the Million Woman March that took place in 1997. The African woman knows that she must continue to challenge White male supremacy in the political and business arena. She is growing sick and tired of her White oppressor believing that *she believes* he is the one most capable of tending to her needs and the needs of her people. This original African mother knows that the oppressor has no monopoly on intelligence and common sense. She also knows that the oppressor severely lacks a moral, humane nature—which is in absolute contradiction to her ancient spirituality.

She shall not be vanquished. Despite the many challenges that face her, the African American woman *still* stands as the ancient symbol of spirituality, dark-skinned beauty, keen intellect, and full figured sensuality. Though not admitted in public, the African woman embodies the standards of spirit, grace, style, and sensuality yearned for by others. Oppressed and envied, she shall not be vanquished.

CHAPTER 2

THE FACE OF AN OLD BLACK WOMAN:
GRANDMOTHERS AND THE STABILITY OF
BLACK FAMILIES

The face of an old Black woman has truths to reveal and lessons to teach. Our old African Queen's sojourn under White supremacy has been a war; her victories are seen in the lives of those Black children and grandchildren she shielded from the poisonous fangs of White supremacy. Those who question the existence of God have only to look into the eyes of our old African Queen; they have only to study the lines of her face. God's presence is seen and felt in the face of an old Black woman.

One feels blessed while in the presence of our old African Queens. We feel strangely safe in her presence and overwhelmingly protective of her. She is in a White male supremacist power structure, the old Black woman has been relegated to nursing homes, where she exists in loneliness as she awaits death, or to the front porch of her earthly dwelling, where she observes life's activities. White supremacy lists her as a medicaid-medicare-social security liability. It doesn't really bother her, though. She simply talks to God, giving thanks for another day and the health of her children. She is our beautiful African Queen.

The old Black woman exists at the margin of White supremacy's society. She was taken for granted by the Whites she slaved for in her youth. She is now ignored by the White power structure that has sapped her physical strength. But through her womb came the fruit of the harvest of African struggle. Maybe this is really why the White power structure despises her: Through her comes the warriors that will challenge and overcome White supremacy. The old Black woman is ancestor-blessed and this makes her a formidable opponent of patriarchal White male supremacy.

There is much to be learned from the old Black woman. Her truths and wisdom are ancient. Her spiritual way of living is a reminder that the spirit existed before religion was born. Her advice is always timely; we all can benefit from listening to her. She can teach young females how to become women and can give advice to boys on becoming men. Remember, she is ancestor-blessed. She is in absolute contrast to the White male power structure. Let us cherish her while we have her.

African American grandmothers are, for many African American families, the great stabilizers. Although my mother and father raised me, my maternal grandmother was the one that looked after us while my parents worked. She was, and still is, loving and firm. My grandmother would make us eat a carrot every day so that we would have "good eyes." And, of course, giving God thanks through prayer was a given. It was not until I matured and began working in the human service profession that I developed an in-depth understanding and appreciation for the roles grandmothers play in the lives of adolescents. Even though things are bad for many African American children, most of them would be going to hell in a handbasket were it not for the limit setting, prayers, and spankings given by grandmothers.

The vast destruction occurring in African American communities—drug and alcohol addictions, teen pregnancy, divorce, unemployment and underemployment, crime, and incarceration—are leading to more and more children, especially those age 6 and under, living with a grandmother and/or grandfather.[1] In 1970, there were 2.2 million American children living in a house that was financially and socially maintained by a grandparent; in 1997 that number rose to 3.9 million children living with grandparents, a 76 percent increase.[2] When these children are living with a grandmother only (as too many African American children are), they are likely to be in dire poverty.[3] Men tend to be major income earners and men tend to be employed longer, but, as a group, African American men don't have long life expectancies and will usually leave a widow who must fend for herself and her grandchild. African American grandmothers and grandfathers form the village that raises the children. I personally know of dozens, perhaps hundreds, of situations in which elderly African American women, some with their daughters, are rearing the children in the grandmother's home.

When I was employed as a youth advocate to work with at-risk youth (majority African American), I had to go into many homes to assess the needs of families. Many of these families, headed primarily by a single mother, were having a hard time with underemployment, a lack of health insurance, and inadequate housing. In many of these families the children, especially if they were adolescent, were having problems at school, thus further complicating the family problems. In roughly half of these families, the grandmother was the moral, financial, nurturing element which held everyone together.

I remember one family that was composed of a single mother, two elementary age children, a middle school aged adolescent, and the maternal grandmother. The mother worked two part-time jobs. The adolescent was having problems at school which centered around his not being able to wear various name-brand clothing. The mother, needless to say, was extremely stressed. Although I was able to work with the young Brother, the degree of progress I made was directly and absolutely the result of the grandmother talking with the Brother. Even at her elderly age, she clearly understood the anguish her grandchild was experiencing. She was empathetic, comforting, and held high expectations (higher than some of his teachers) for her grandchild. I was able to reach him because she was able to reach him. This teen's improvement at school removed some of the stress placed on his mother. The grandmother's presence in that home was spiritual. As with all African American grandmothers, she prayed daily, thanking God for strength and asking God to look after the family. I am convinced that no social service agency can provide the kind of guidance and motivation that comes so easily to African American grandmothers.

Here is an experience that shows what can happen in the absence of the spiritual, stabilizing grandmother figure. I was working with a very bright 14 year-old who would frequently skip school and had begun to sell crack. Initially, he lived with his mother and three younger siblings. After mom got tired of having to leave work to go talk to her son's principal, she sent him to live with her mother. For the first time, I was now able to make some progress with the Brother. Grandmother was very concerned about her grandson, and since she was retired, had time to talk to him and take him places. His school life became more stable and I was going to help him get summer employment. But, unbeknownst to me and his grandmother, all along he had been asking his mother to allow him to come back home. Mom gave in, and it was downhill from there. While mother was at work, he would get with some friends and male relatives and help them sell crack. He was eventually murdered.

Many of the "old" grandmothers possess what I like to call pre-desegregation values. These were the old-fashioned beliefs and behaviors that were the standard of African American behavior. These standards, based on morals, spirituality, and common sense, demanded respect for life, self, and others. So, when an African American family is blessed to have a grandmother present, it has a greater chance of weathering the many storms that White supremacy brings its way. Even with both mother and father present, it is always helpful to have extended families. The American habit of throwing away the elderly is something that too many African Americans have begun to do. Whether parent or grandparent, too many of us view the elderly as a nuisance and will diligently seek a nursing home to have them placed. We seldom stop to think that we are literally throwing away an invaluable human resource. A friend's mother experienced a stroke and had to be placed in a nursing home. She is not doing well and has been in the nursing home for two years now. He visits her *every* day! He has a bedroom at his home ready for his mother when she is released from the nursing home. This is an example of the spirit of unity that is so badly needed in African American communities.

It is always comforting for both child and adult to arrive home after school or work, knowing that their gray-haired, praying, ready-to-help grandmother is there. The face of an old Black woman is a physical reminder of what we Africans in America had lost and must regain—especially if we are to overcome White supremacy.

CHAPTER 3

NATIVE AMERICAN WOMEN, OTHER WOMEN, WHITE WOMEN

"When I look back now from this high hill of my old age, I can still see the butchered women and children lying heaped and scattered all along the crooked gulch...And I can see that something else died there in the bloody mud, and was buried in the blizzard. A people's dream died there. It was a beautiful dream..."

Black Elk (quoted from *Bury My Heart At Wounded Knee*)

"While persons we classify as black or white still comprise America's major races, they currently account for a smaller share of the population than at any time in our history. . . In many respects, other groups find themselves sitting as spectators, while the two prominent players try to work out how or whether they can coexist with one another."[1]

The trials and tribulations faced by African American women must not be viewed in absolute isolation, even though, as Frances Cress Welsing warns in *The Isis Papers*, African people are the main target of White supremacy. Other women of color have also faced the brutal reality of patriarchal White male supremacist aggression, and this reality gives most women of color a common enemy. While African American women must not naively believe that all other women of color are in agreement with stopping White supremacy, they must form alliances with those who agree that patriarchal White male supremacy is the root cause of their oppression.

She is Navaho, Sioux, Apache, Ute, Yamacraw, Comanche, Cheyenne, Kiowa, and many more. She has witnessed the Godless, brutal assault of White male supremacy firsthand. The Native American woman has looked into the hate filled eyes of Satan and has seen his blood-stained hands. She saw her father, husband, and son stand bravely before the demonic invaders. And she saw them fall.

This mother experiences daily reminders of the oppression of her people. White male supremacy has placed her people in a dungeon of despair. On her land and in her home, she is a victim. The wounded spirit of her people is reflected in the numerous ills facing them. Her heart breaks as she yearns for a better life for her children. She, more than anyone else, knows the *true* history of America, and it is a history that reads like a nightmare. It is a history of murder, rape, and broken hearts.

Native American women must become key players in women's struggle for self-determination. The historical and present-day truth of the trials and tribulations of her people are best articulated by her. No one can express the pain of a people better than a mother. She should also be the one to state the demands of her people. Native American and African American women have gone from the frying pan into the fire and back again. Each of these women has experienced a holocaust. Any serious self-determination plan must include the most oppressed of the oppressed!

The very words "Native American" or "Indian," bring to mind images of betrayal, genocide, and a people done wrong. This woman is a visual and spiritual reminder of the millions who are now extinct because of the greed and immorality of the patriarchal White male power structure.

Her ancestors live through her, and she has much to contribute to the struggle.

Korean, Chinese, East Indian, Japanese, Palestinian, Arabian, and other nonwhite women in America are, in varying degrees, victims of patriarchal White male supremacist socialization. Through colonization and imperialism, White male governments, military, religious organizations, and corporations forced their values and lifestyles onto others. Although the majority of these women function from a tribal, ethnic group orientation that is based on nonwhite, nonwestern values, more and more of them seek to obtain a Caucasian lifestyle. They imitate the exploited American White woman, much like some of their African American and other Sisters of color. Through their imitation and worship of White women, they are placed directly under the control of the White male supremacist power structure. In some ways, White women are the bait that is used to lure nonwhites into the jaws of White male supremacy.

The pathetic but profitable image of the White female as being every man's desire have blinded other women to the truth about the status of the American White woman: Prostituted and abused by White male corporate America. These women can't see the forest because of the trees of White illusion and mental conditioning. Although most women of color remain well connected to their ethnic group and its values, many rapidly jump into the White male supremacist's pool of illusion.

Many Chinese, Palestinian, Korean, Arab, Japanese, and other nonwhite women fervently seek to acquire the physical characteristics and demeanor of White women. The deeper these women get into their imitation of White women, the further removed they become from their ethnic/ cultural group, and their sense of self. They too become a Frankenstein creation with someone else's thoughts, eye color, hair color, facial features and body size. Their wife-husband relationships will start to deteriorate as they become entrenched in the patriarchal White male supremacist created madness. Corruption, perversion, and destruction will become the order of their illusion filled days.

Entire nonwhite cultures are assimilated and evaporated after they walk through the doors of a morally and spiritually void White supremacist social structure. The inherent dysfunctionality of White supremacy is a cancer that eats away the common sense and cultural values these women were born into. Eating disorders and substance abuse, blond-dyed hair and size two jeans, disrespectful children and hundreds of hours of television—unknowing victims of Godless rulers.

These other women, through their assimilation of White values, may also adopt the racial views of Whites, especially some Whites' negative views of African Americans, Native Americans, and Latino Americans. When other women adopt White supremacist views of many people of color, they are also participating in the oppression of other people of color. Like some White women, they too have become assistant oppressors. Once they deteriorate to the level of assistant oppressors, Arabs, Koreans, Chinese, Japanese, East Indians and others begin to treat their Sisters and Brothers of color as inferior beings. The men fight like crabs in a barrel for scraps of power, and the women keep their distance from other women of color. As a result, these women suffer a strange mixture of cultural amnesia, schizophrenia, and self-doubt.

Native American Women, Other Women,
White Women

The White woman's life is a paradox. While she is numero uno partner of the White man, she is simultaneously his victim. It is the White woman who receives the spoils of the White man's conquests and, in perverted fashion, became his abused plaything---pampered and pimped, cuddled and beaten, placed on a pedestal and dropped in the gutter.

To a greater and lesser extent, White women have always supported White men. bell hooks states:

> It is usually materially privileged white women who identify as feminists, and who have gained greater social equality and power with white men in the existing social structure, who resist most vehemently the revolutionary feminist insistence that an anti-racist agenda must be at the core of our movement if there is ever to be solidarity between women and effective coalitions thatcross racial boundaries and unite us in common struggle.[2]

Even when White women challenge the White male created status-quo and seriously annoy the White male power structure, she is patronized and redirected. Their relationship with White men, along with their own whiteness, places White women in an awkward position when it comes to dealing with the destructive exploitation of the patriarchal White male power structure. She is faced with the fact that she must confront and challenge her son, husband, brother, and lover if she is to stop her crucifixion. Literally speaking, she must fight within her household if she is to reach her human potential.

White women have been made the most valued and most prostituted women on earth. She has been placed on a pedestal then stripped of her clothes by her man, who then sells her to the highest bidder. Her White mate sells her to both legitimate and illegitimate enterprises. Although other groups have, to their detriment, imitated Whites, it is a sign of madness that they would imitate a woman who has been prostituted in order to sell magazines, videos, cars, shampoo, dog food, clothing, guns, and every other item. For the White man, the White woman is only as valuable as her potential to be exploited and prostituted.

In assessing her relationship with other women, the White woman must confront her whiteness. This is necessary because her whiteness often determines, consciously and subconsciously, the degree of equality, oneness, and togetherness she feels with women of color. White women must ask themselves, "What does my whiteness mean to me?" And "Am I better than women of color or equal to them?" Such self-examination is necessary if White women are to sincerely become part of a movement that is determined to end female exploitation by the White male power structure. This White male power structure has mandated that White women "Be as I am and what I want you to be when I want you to be it." Whether a White woman is an ultra-liberal feminist or a confederate flag waving neo-nazi, they both must redefine themselves in terms of their relationship to nonwhite people and powerful White men if they are truly to be liberated.

It is the White woman who, through her actions, must become the apologetic and redeeming conscience of the White race. The awesome task of assisting oppressed women of color to end their oppression will be a sobering task for most White women. White women will be welcomed with open arms, as long as they do not conduct themselves in a mother-knows-best manner, acting as if her Sisters of color are less capable of carrying out the task of liberation. Equality must be practiced, not preached.

In a true liberation movement, White women will always be faced with the charge of treason. White men will not let her change sides so easily; they are used to her disagreeing with them or attacking them simply because she *wants to be like them.*

> No doubt white patriarchal men must have found it amusing and affirming that many of the white women who had so vehemently and fiercely denounced domination were quite happy to assume the role of oppressor and/or exploiter if it meant that they could wield power equally with white men.[3]

White women will constantly be faced with the decision to either continue with her Sisters of color or go back to being a pampered and prostituted money maker for the patriarchal White male supremacist system. It will be tough, but she is capable of morally and spiritually redeeming the blood-stained hands of her man.

Comprehending and connecting across racial and economic lines is necessary for women to wrench themselves free of patriarchal White supremacy. Women must not allow themselves to be distracted from the goal of ending White supremacy. Patriarchal White supremacy compromises nothing, and women must be clear on this fact. Those women who are awaiting rewards for the patriarchal White power structure must examine themselves. If they find that they can't resist the "30 pieces of silver" they should simply step aside and not hinder those women seeking liberation from the patriarchal White power structure. Since Native American and African American women have experienced the most brutal assault by White men, they should take the lead in setting and implementing the plan of action. In essence, women must act as a tribe (possessing common goals and ideas) in checkmating patriarchal White supremacy.

CHAPTER 4

MYTH OF THE "UGLY BODY"

Who are those glamour queens in size two jeans? Making me look in the mirror And hate what I see Making me eat rice cakes And whatever it takes To be like those glamour queens in size two jeans...

Excerpted from Nathalie Gottlieb's
Glamour Queens in Size Two Jeans

She thinks her brown body Has no glory. If she could dance Naked, Under palm trees, And see her image in the river She would know.

Waring Cuney's *No Images*

The worst form of female crucifixion is self-hate. Every woman in America is a victim of a White male supremacist, self-hate instilling socialization. From the cradle to the grave, American and many other Western women are taught to be displeased with their weight or skin color or hair texture or hair length or breast size or eye color or nose and lip size. In *Black Looks: Race and Representation*, author bell hooks describes how loving blackness is hazardous in a "white supremacist culture,"[1] to the point where death is the punishment. While teaching a course on Black women writers, she says that "It became painfully obvious by the lack of response that this group of diverse students (many of them black people) were more interested in discussing the desire of black folks to be white, indeed were fixated on this issue."[2] hooks mentions that White supremacy has impacted African Americans so much that we often find it difficult to discuss "loving blackness."[3]

75

From an early age, females are socialized through a demonic marketing concept to create, in their minds, the ideal female image, and then spend the rest of their lives trying to transform themselves into that ideal image. These female victims embark on a frustrating and sometimes deadly journey that put them at the mercy of fads, gimmicks, con artists, and guinea pigism—all of which make money off women and provide only temporary satisfaction, if any.

> Early on, business leaders realized that in order to make people "want" things they had never previously desired, they had to create "the dissatisfied consumer.". . .The key to economic prosperity is the organized creation of dissatisfaction.[4]

The above statement reveals much about the rationale behind the madness that affects and effects all of America and much of the world. No longer content to create dissatisfaction with competing products, marketing now seeks to make people dissatisfied with themselves. This is especially true of women. The psychological and emotional state of such marketing induced self-dissatisfaction, before leading to self-hate, changes a person into a *thing*. The immoral White male supremacist rulers have created a self-hate instilling marketing scheme that has transformed women into products seeking the ultimate product—the ideal physical female body. Although all women in America are victims of this self-dissatisfaction to some degree, it is necessary to separately explain the effects of this madness on African American women and White women—the two historical players on this tragic stage.

African American women were victims of White male supremacist instilled self-hate long before the 1920s.

The African woman's body was used as a public restroom by White men. She was simultaneously despised, lusted after, and raped by White men. Although her Black skin and full figure were historical symbols of beauty, she was placed in the nonhuman category by racist power holders who, nonetheless, desired her and used her for sexual entertainment. What one must realize is that the African/ African American woman was never a standard of beauty in American society. The instilling of self-hate for the African American woman began in the holes of Western slave ships.

The lusciousness of her full lips, the voluptuousness of her full figure, the richness of her dark eyes, and the delightful texture of her hair were purposely degraded and made "ugly" by patriarchal White male society. Queen Latifah states:

> I'm about being healthy. And, according to my doctor, I can be healthy at two hundred pounds. And you know when you're healthy. You don't have to go on some crash diet, drink Slim Fast every day, and go crazy to lose weight. I'm not for that. I'm about feeling good at whatever size I am.[5]

Keeping in mind that everyone cannot have and should not have the same weight, it is important to note that if African American women are to obtain and maintain their health, which is crucial, they must be mindful of their weight.

> Obesity is rising among all minorities, but one of the more mysterious health statistics to emerge from a decade's worth of research conducted at the Centers for Disease Control and Prevention shows that weight gain is most likely among black women between the ages of

twenty-five and thirty-four. Indeed, at every age, black women are significantly more likely to be obese than any other group.[6]

Obesity carries with it a variety of deadly diseases such as Type II diabetes, hypertension, stroke, and heart disease.[7] Although the cause of obesity among African American women in their prime years is unknown, researchers generally point to diet as the reason.[8] It is common for many African Americans, both female and male, to eat a meal consisting of rice (red or white), potato salad, macaroni and cheese, several pieces of fried meat, only one serving of vegetable, and a slice of cake or pie. Although these meals are delicious (trust me, I was reared on these meals), they can be deadly if they are overindulged. The quality of what is eaten is sometimes overlooked as people tend to focus on taste and quantity. It is easy to eat a great deal of nothing. For instance, a pregnant woman may eat large portions of food daily, but the child can end up undernourished because the food consumed by the mother lacked nutritive value; the result, and this is interesting, can be obesity in the unborn child's later years[9]. Many physicians and other health specialists also point to the role of diet in preventing breast and uterine fibroid tumors.

Risk factors that contribute to fibroid development include the use of high-estrogen birth-control pills, estrogen replacement therapy in postmenopausal women with pre-existing fibroids, obesity, family history, B-vitamin deficiency, significant emotional or physical stress and a diet characterized by excessive alcohol, fat, red meat, dairy products, chocolate and sugar, according to Lark.[10]

Both breast and uterine fibroids mainly affect females between the ages of 20 and 50.[11] I am personally amazed and frightened by the large numbers of women in their early 20s who have or had uterine fibroid tumors. The necessity of eating nutritiously and exercising regularly is quite evident. I remember commenting to a female relative about her eating habits and weight gain. Her response to me was, "My husband likes it!" She was being defensive but I knew that she was concerned. Women must be healthy for themselves and their young children, not for Mr. Right, because only about 10 percent of African American men ages 20 to 44 are overweight.[12] Eating nutritiously is matter of life and death. Even stress is alleviated through exercise and nutritious eating. Women must maintain excellent health if they are to be successful in fighting patriarchal White supremacy. And remember: White supremacy's attack is both physical and psychological, with especially devastating impacts on African American women.

For more than two centuries, the African/African American woman has been vitiated by the White male power structure. So, who became the standard of beauty for African/African American women? White women.

Television, print media, classroom textbooks, and the Bible (Eurocentric versions) have, for centuries, presented White women as angelic beauties and damsels in distress. White women were the fair maidens placed on a pedestal for all to worship and adore. Long straight hair, tiny noses, thin lips, and light colored eyes became the ideal female image in the minds of many oppressed, miseducated African/African American women and men. While White women were being elevated to the heights of goddesses, African/African American women were simultaneously denigrated. As a result of White supremacist oppression and miseducation, light complexioned African/African American women became "pretty" and dark complexioned Sisters became "ugly." Black women with long, straight hair and light complexions were standards of beauty in most, if not all, African American communities. Many African American women used skin bleaching creams and hair straightening products in the sad attempt to come as close as possible in physical appearance to White women.

As time progressed, wearing blue contact lenses, dyeing dark hair blond, and, for those who could afford it, undergoing plastic surgery was added to the African/African American woman's list of how to become a White woman. Still today, the voluptuous figure, sensuously full lips, and lovely hair texture of African American women are ignored and down-played by the White owned and operated electronic and print media. African Americans must take control of representing our image, and stop expecting Whites to positively present us to the world. The more Black women run away from their African selves to a nonAfrican self, the greater the likelihood of acquiring destructive beliefs and behaviors. When I worked as an educational therapist for a private psychiatric hospital, I attended a seminar on eating disorders—anorexia nervosa and bulimia. The psychiatrists conducting the workshop stated that there were no documented cases of African American and Latino women with eating disorders (this was during the early 80s). If you researched the number of African American women suffering from eating disorders today, you would be amazed. Clearly, African American women are imitating White women to *death*. Let us now examine White women.

White women have been tossed from one extreme to the other by the patriarchal White male power structure. She was once the flawless beauty but has now become a conditional beauty—the condition being that of thinness and a willingness to have her body surgically altered. White male power holders form and reform the White woman's body in accordance to the profit they wish to accrue. The desirability of the White woman has gone from the fullness of Marilyn Monroe to the current emaciated anorexic. White women are conditioned to undergo cosmetic surgery and to receive silicone injections more than any other women. White men decide how White women should look and, through their media, they instruct White women to change their bodies. Many White women are literally dying to please White men. From cradle to grave, White women are pressured into becoming a Barbie doll or the latest, very thin, entertainment attraction. Judging from media depictions, the White male power structure currently prefers pencil thin White women with large breasts.

As long as White women shape themselves into the images created by emotionally cold, insecure, greedy White male power holders, they will suffer. Schizophrenic and sadistic White males have seduced White women into a twisted game of "Simon Says."

The image of the "ugly" body will forever torment American women as long as they allow themselves to be duped by the madness and marketing of the patriarchal White male power structure. Women are not automobiles whose bodies conform to the stroke of a designer's pencil and then put on display for potential buyers to. Women must cease the destructive and unnecessary dieting, skin-bleaching, skin-tanning, plastic surgery, silicone injections, and starvation that they have been programmed to put themselves through or they will self-destruct. Again, women must realize that their marketing induced self-hatred is profitable for the White male power structure. If someone wants you to become the myth that exists in his mind, you can only satisfy that person by discontinuing to exist because myths are fiction; in other words, you must cease living in order to satisfy the myth holder.

CHAPTER 5

LOVE OR LUST?

Western ideology and practice have marketed, socialized, programmed, politicized, and otherwise condemned women to be the receptacles of the most base male habits. In other words, a woman is worthwhile only to the degree she's being lusted after. A woman that does not attract male lust is, theoretically, punished by ostracization. The White male power holders have made all of society an auction block for the women of the world. An auction block where females must exhibit their bodies for the entertainment of men and submission to the highest bidders.

The marketing and socialization of women as sexual objects contribute to the destruction of marriages, communities, and eventually nations. A man cannot simultaneously care for a woman as an object of lust and as a human being. This is impossible. The control oriented mentality of the global patriarchal White male supremacist power structure has instilled, in too many males, the belief that to mentally, emotionally, and spiritually love a woman is taboo. The destructiveness of such teachings in the lives of men and women cannot be emphasized enough. A real man must never be genuine—he must fake it; he must deceive. A real man doesn't tell his peers how much he loves a woman—only how she is in bed. A real man won't have a woman who earns more than he earns (this is especially sensitive for some members of oppressed groups such African Americans and Latinos).

While women are open to establishing meaningful relationships that can lead to marriage, miseducated men are seeking a relationship of dominance. The sexist/racist teachings of the White male power structure are so ingrained in men that many of those who truly want to have a genuine, sharing relationship often experience feelings of embarrassment, fear, and anger. I believe that many men become physically and emotionally abusive to women because they are afraid and repulsed by their suppressed thoughts and feelings of caring. Such men are sick. A society whose rulers teach and condone the subjugation and exploitation of women will be riddled with conflict, abuse, drug addiction, murder, and a high divorce rate. The polarization of women and men in American society is an offshoot of the insecure, paranoid, hostile White supremacist ideology of this nation's power structure. The fact that large numbers of their racial group is being destroyed is of little concern to them. Interpersonal turmoil among women and men is used as a divide and rule strategy by the patriarchal power structure.

The idea of love between women and men carries the historical belief that this will lead to marriage. This idea and historical belief of love and marriage are what builds and maintains families and nations. Marriage lays the foundation for the building of families. It is normal and healthy for women and men to want to marry and produce children. However, when a man believes in the suppression and exploitation of women, problems develop in the relationship. When a man believes that women are placed on earth by God for the purpose of sexually entertaining men, serious problems develop. When men believe that it is alright to be with a woman and not care about her, problems develop. When a woman is trying to develop a sharing/caring relationship while the man is developing a control/deceit based relationship, they will end up with no relationship. The result of this madness is that quite often, the woman ends up a mother with only her child.

Love is incompatible with subjugation, deceit, lust, and insecurity. The chauvinistic paternalism of the White male power structure is incompatible with love. Control, domination, and exploitation are all the power holders know. In essence, American society and other Westernized societies become more anti-family with each passing decade. The policies, practices, and structure of American society are not conducive to women and men becoming wives and husbands. How can a society that socializes boys and girls to become ruthless, individualistic competitors ever have successful wife-husband relationships? Too many women and men become frustrated with one another. Penis-vagina based relationships amount to little more than pimp-prostitute business transactions. Nobody wins; the children and women lose.

In "A Matter of Trust," singer Billy Joel tells the truth: "Some love is just a lie of the soul, the constant battle for the ultimate state of control," and "Some love is just a lie of the heart, the cold remains of what began with a passionate start," and "Some love is just a lie of the mind, it's make believe until it's only just a matter of time." African Philosopher Malidoma Some' stated that in his village of Burkina Faso, West Africa, people marry before falling in love. Dr. Some' compared starting out a life together in love (which is the Western preference) to being on top of a mountain—you can't go any higher. However, if a couple starts at the bottom of the mountain, there's only one way to go—up. Under a system of patriarchal White male supremacy, however, both men and women, boys and girls, are socialized to lie, pretend, and dominate, and this is called "love."

The White male power structure cannot comprehend, cannot be physically seen, heard, touched, or tasted. This had led to their conjuring up what they think of love. Their love, though, is lust-filled, competition-based madness. Under their pathological social programming, a man's "love" for a woman is only as great as his lust for her—the greater his erection, the greater is his "love." So, when his lustful fires have been quenched, the love is gone. The woman is tossed aside like a used napkin.

Women must teach men and their children the distinction between lust and love. Women must teach their families how to love. Love making begins in the heart, proceeds to the mind, and concludes in the genital organs. Women must teach men to make love to their spirit and mind. You will know the depth of a man's love by the quality of his listening.

PART THREE

AGENCIES AND INSTITUTIONS

CHAPTER 1

ZERO TOLERANCE FOR BLACK SKIN:
AFRICAN AMERICAN WOMEN BEHIND BARS

African American women have joined their men on the new slave plantations—America's prison system. With more than one million people imprisoned, this institution, more than any other under patriarchal White supremacy, is being tailored for African Americans. The one investment that local, state, and federal governments are willing to make in African Americans is the building of prisons. Although many people are aware of the huge number of African American males imprisoned, many people are just becoming aware of the high number of African American females that are warehoused in America's newest slave plantations.

Many people's eyes were opened about the horrors of African American mothers, daughters, and wives behind bars when *Emerge* published "Kemba's Nightmare" in May 1996, and again with part two (Kemba's Nightmare Part II in May 1998). Kemba Smith's tragic story awakened many people to the unfairness that exists in America's prison/plantation/concentration camp system. It is no secret that African Americans are more likely to be sentenced, and are given longer sentences than other groups, including Whites. African American women, however, are twice victimized. She is first victimized because she is African. Since the ending of the European slave trade, America has developed zero tolerance for African Americans. The Black woman, once valued as a mammy and a tool for the slave master's sexual gratification, is now, along with her man, an unwanted element in American society. The African American woman is also victimized because she is a woman. She is victimized by White and sadly, some African American men. Women are raped and sexually assaulted, beaten, and terrorized more than men.[1] According to the U.S. Department of Justice's Bureau of Justice Statistics, females were about two-thirds as likely as males to be victims of violence while 20 years prior, females were only half as likely as males to be victims of violence.[2] These sad statistics mirror the inherent anti-female (especially anti-Black female) philosophy and structure of patriarchal White supremacist society.

Several other factors must be viewed when examining the large and rapidly increasing number of African American women behind bars: drug use, drug selling, low income and the decline of husbands and fathers.

During my experience as a family and child therapist and an educational therapist, I learned that most African Americans who use drugs do so to escape from emotional and mental pain. While many Whites use drugs for recreational purposes, most African Americans do not. Most of the African American female addicts that I have counseled were single, poor mothers living in economically depressed communities. Some were as young as 16 years of age and others 50 years and older. All were good people and wonderful mothers until they developed the disease of addiction. Therapy sessions focused on helping the mothers develop spiritually-based inner strength; placing them in a support group; helping them locate a job; and helping them to become involved in wholesome activities such as volunteering to assist in after school programs, singing in a church choir, or taking business classes.

When the women began to feel better about themselves and their social situation, then progress occurred.

It is no secret that parents feel good when they can provide a decent life for their children. The patriarchal White supremacist knows this, too. White supremacy is well aware of what makes a healthy, productive community and what can destroy a community. It is a diabolical process that goes like this: First, devalue Black skin; second, create governmental and corporate policies that go against the well being of African Americans; third, miseducate African Americans by teaching them a European-based curriculum that discourages self-sufficiency; fourth, psychologically frustrate and incarcerate African American men so that only females are left to parent the children; fifth , remove all businesses such as grocery stores, shopping centers, and hospitals far away from majority African American communities; and sixth, flood African American communities with crack cocaine and liquor stores. I am personally and professionally convinced that African American communities will experience a tremendous decrease in crack addiction if these destructive elements are checkmated. Needless to say, African American women must launch a no-holds-barred, no-nonsense approach to alleviate these genocidal conditions. Anyone who does not help African American women, either directly or indirectly, is directly harming African American women. In light of the present conditions, how can it be viewed any other way?

A very tragic dynamic exists among children whose mothers are crack addicted. These children are angry, *very* angry. Many children of addicted mothers are checked (teased) by their peers at school and in the neighborhood.

My most challenging cases were the children of addicted mothers. Understand: Many crack addicted females turn to shoplifting and prostitution to finance their habit. It is quite common for the prostitution to take place in the neighborhood near crack houses; therefore, the child and peers often witness the solicitation. Extreme anger, hurt, and embarrassment are the emotions experienced by these children on a daily basis. Still these children love their addicted mothers. I teach the children about the causes of addiction and what we African people must do to stop this madness. Our children need to know the truth about African American women and men using crack, drinking a 40-ounces, and other alcoholic beverages. When children are taught the environmental-social-economic-psychological aspects of using drugs, they are much less likely to use drugs, and are more likely to realize the need to change conditions in the African American community.

People who sell drugs, including African American women, sell drugs for money. The African American women imprisoned in America for selling drugs are mostly poor and acquired no wealth from dealing drugs. These are overwhelmingly poor women from poor communities, and poor communities have the worst of everything, including drug arrests and crime:

> Persons from households with lower incomes were more vulnerable to violent crime than those from higher income households. Persons with household incomes of less than $35,000 per year had significantly higher violent crime rates for the category of total violent crime when compared with those who had household incomes of $35,000 or more per year.[3]

Zero Tolerance for Black Skin:
African American Women Behind Bars

Poor African American communities that have large numbers of female headed households and unemployed men and teens are a cocaine producer's dream. Some of the oppressed and depressed African Americans will try to escape via crack cocaine while others seek to obtain the American Dream by selling crack. The June 2000 issue of *Ebony*, states the problem:

> Thousands of Black women are serving long sentences because of zero tolerance policies and mandatory sentences connected to America's war on drugs. Experts believe this "war" is largely responsible for the doubling of the female prison population over the last 10 years and the disproportionate incarceration rate for African-American women.[4]

The only war taking place in America is the war on Black folk. The patriarchal White supremacist power structure created the conditions that lead to African American female imprisonment, and the fact that they lock people up to supposedly stop drug selling and drug use proves that they have no interest in stopping *African Americans* from using and selling drugs. White supremacy cannot and will not examine the cause of African American female incarceration. The African American community must, again, develop a plan to save itself. In a nation where the female prison population grew 75 percent between 1986 and 1991, it would be suicidal to wait on this very system to save African Americans.[5] More current data reveals that at year-end 1999 (December 31, 1999), the number of females in state and federal prisons increased 4.4 percent, to 90,668, rapidly outpacing male incarceration, which rose by 3.3 percent.[6] African Americans must have zero faith in the racist prison system that has become America's new slave plantation. The development of family-educational-vocational support structures by African American women for African American women are crucial.

CHAPTER 2

THE POLITICAL PIMPING OF WOMEN

The political institution must definitely be discussed. It is through political validation or invalidation that people are made to be viewed as valuable or worthless by society. It is against this institution, governed by White patriarchs, that women must fight.

Two significant points are revealed in chapter 9 of Angela Y. Davis' *Women Race & Class*. The first is that there is an absolute relationship between politics and employment. Second, when the women's suffrage movement began in the late 1860s, Susan B. Anthony and Elizabeth Cady Stanton never embraced "the fundamental principles of unity and class solidarity, without which the labor movement would remain powerless."[1] It is necessary to state these points for two reasons: First, politics is about the allocation/creation of monetary access/privilege, and the ultimate obtainment of power—power to become self-determined. Second, some White women will exclude or exploit their Sisters of color while pretending to be for all women and against any kind of exploitation/racism. Their true agenda is camouflaged behind a mask of deceit. There must be no camouflaging of agendas if women are to end the political pimping. African American, Native American, European American, Latino/Hispanic, Asian American and other women must be synchronized in their understanding, planning, and implementation if this planet is to be freed from White supremacist oppression.

Women vote frequently and in large numbers. Politicians know this. The most powerful politicians are able to stay in power because of votes received from exploited, subjugated women, thus creating one of the more interesting ironies in American life—the exploited helping their exploiters remain in power. Patriarchal logic is that women aren't intelligent enough or psychologically strong enough to conduct political affairs. The only role women are encouraged to play is that of keeping men, mainly White men, in power. This is the reality despite the fact that there are very influential female politicians.

Within the political context, patriarchal White male supremacy unintentionally defines itself through its belief that women are incapable of handling political affairs. If patriarchal-based politics is a ruthless, deceitful, immoral practice that women are not, by nature, able to implement, then White men must be able to implement these policies because they are naturally ruthless, deceitful, and immoral. Women and oppressed men should never imitate nor emulate such men. Imitation would merely result in substituting one form of oppression for another.

The political pimps approach women from a biological and economic standpoint. The woman's body is used as a political football. Should she or should she not be allowed by White men to have an abortion? Should she or should she not be given the opportunity to earn the salaries White men earn? Should she or should she not be given medical care for herself and her children? The White male gods of patriarchy sit on their thrones and make life and death decisions for women. These decisions are sometimes based less on what women truly need or want but more on what patriarchal propaganda has convinced women to believe they need and want. In this scenario, women are sometimes pitted against one another in a game that is always won by the White male power structure. White women must be careful not to become assistant oppressors and women of color must be careful not to become cheap, psychotic, money hungry imitators of their oppressor.

Election year campaigns bring forth power crazed White men propagandizing, patronizing, begging, and lying to women in a manner that will amaze professional con artists. The women of the Democratic, Republican, Independent, or other parties are equally conned. Social-political television talk shows repeatedly air the opinions of White male professionals about issues that pertain to women. Middle-aged, wealthy, White male patriarchs passionately and hypocritically inform women about the wonderful changes that await them if they are elected to various offices. What is baffling about this is the fact that women repeatedly vote their oppressors into office, thus perpetuating female oppression. With empty promises of child care availability, employee rights, medical benefits, and increased employment opportunities, women, like oppressed nonwhite men, simply lose their rational abilities, mesmerized by the world's most notorious promise breakers.

If, as Niccolo Machiavelli stated, politics is in no way related to morals, then women can only expect more lies, bitterness, and frustration. This is made worse because many women are mothers, and when their lives are hindered their children suffer. Seldom do women suffer in isolation. With the large number of single mothers in America, issues of children, health insurance, job security, and job flexibility become more crucial. The White male patriarchal power structure *enjoys* the exacerbation of women's issues because they can use the promise of resolving these issues (which they created) to further manipulate women during political campaigns. Patriarchal White male supremacists know how to instill hope into oppressed people and then manipulate their hopes for the benefit of White male power. The victims' hopes tend to last the duration of the politician's stay in office.

I must state here that nonwhite male politicians sometimes utilize the same ruthless strategies as White men in dealing with women. These nonwhite men are merely childish imitators of White men; they have no true power, only the very limited authority White men allow them to have. Since these nonwhite men fervently seek the approval and monetary crumbs the White male patriarchs throw them (for helping to oppress their own people), African American and Latino women can expect no support from them whatsoever. Having compromised their integrity, these men are now being pimped by their oppressor.

When Europeans fled and were forced out of Europe, they brought their Protestant beliefs about women with them to the lands they conquered. Under Protestantism, women were only fit to bear children and perform domestic chores. Period.[2] The present White male patriarchal power structure has as its reference point, a very long, religion-validated history of subjugating women. Where is a "woman's place?" The answer is: Wherever White men say her place is. The White male patriarchal politician believes that he is the most qualified person to tell women what they need, want, and who is to provide these needs and wants. The White patriarch is the premier pimp in a sadistic game of political prostitution, and he's selling promises of a brighter tomorrow.

The fact that the United States Government and most major American corporations are headed by White men is no coincidence. It is testimony to the white male belief that women are incapable of holding positions of power. These men realize, however, the significance of manipulating issues to secure the votes of women. Women must learn how to use their voting strength for their overall benefit.

CHAPTER 3

MYTH OF THE POWERLESS WOMAN

In comprehending the disastrous impact of patriarchal White supremacy in the lives of women, it is necessary to examine the harmful reality of myths embodied in the rules and regulations of every agency and institution created, operated, and controlled by White men. Every institution established by the patriarchal White power structure contains and functions under various myths pertaining to women. A woman can be a bank teller but not the bank president. A woman can be the crying mother or wife who waves goodbye to her soldier son/husband, but she cannot be the soldier. She can be the corporate accountant but not the corporation's chief executive officer. For the African American woman, the myths are even more damaging. African American women are viewed as inferior not simply because of their womanhood, but because they are African. All the negative stereotypes of African people (being lazy, dumb, and childlike) are added to the general myths regarding women, thus placing a tremendous mental, emotional, spiritual burden on African American women. For example, Anita Allen's experience reveals that even educational achievements mean very little in the educational institutions (in this case, Carnegie Mellon University) of the White power structure:

> And not that the academic environment was always supportive. At one point, as a doctoral candidate and teaching fellow, she was confronted by a young white man who demanded to know, "What gives you the right to teach this class?" She assumed a similar challenge would not have been made had she been male and white.

. . . . "I'm not sure you have the power we're looking for," she recalls him saying, in assessing her intellectual ability and drive.[1]

The patriarchal White power structure cannot endure the spirit and mentality of a Harriet Tubman, Queen Nzinga, Sojourner Truth, Queen Hatshepsut, Mary McLeod Bethune, Fannie Lou Hamer, and Rosa Parks. Such feminine power is feared by the patriarchal White power structure. Thus, White male rulers developed a definition of feminine as beautiful and virtuous and lacking strength and power. The servile, docile woman, much like the subservient slave mammy, is the shining example of womanhood. Women who are obedient and submissive to White male authority are true women, the women of choice. So, like children, women were to be seen and not heard, patronized and tolerated but never taken seriously.

Needless to say, the submissive, docile woman will be eternally exploited by the patriarchal White power structure. The African American woman, especially, will exist in a living hell; for it is she who, more than any other woman, *must* develop and act upon strength of mind, spirit, and character. The African American woman must be the warrior queen whose spirit absolutely defies the rulership of White supremacy.

Actual powerlessness exists when the so-called powerless believe they are indeed powerless. The belief often exists before the condition. At the heart of power is self-determination. When people plan, set, and implement their own agendas they are self-determining. When others plan, set, and implement their agendas for *your* group, you are simply being colonized. Many people of color understand colonization all too well. It is necessary that women, too, understand this.

Women and African people are targeted for the worst kind of powerlessness—that of being *naturally* powerless. Although this type of powerlessness does not exist in scientific terms, it is very much a part of White male supremacy's historic, traditional belief system. This type of thinking is passed along from generation to generation and is ingrained in every institution under White male supremacy control, including government, industry, military, and academia. To be female under White male supremacy is to be inferior.

Fearful, insecure men have serious problems with women. With all the economic, military, and political power at their disposal white males still feel fearful and insecure. Their "male versus female ideology has influenced many men to fear and feel insecure about women. This twisted practice and ideology makes White male supremacists feel "normal" and comfortable in "knowing" that other men feel as they do about women. Nonwhite men don't realize that they are conditioned, like guinea pigs, to believe and behave according to the dictates of the mad mind of White male supremacy. The more powerless women believe they are, the more powerless women will become. Passive women, especially passivity nonwhite women, are the White supremacist's dream. The White male power structure knows that there is a direct correlation between the passiveness of women and the oppression of their men. If women fight injustice, their men cannot stand idly by. Women—mothers, wives, daughters—give men every reason to put their lives on the line because true men endeavor to provide, protect, and defend their families. Assertive female behavior is not desired under patriarchal White male supremacy. Women must not be allowed to become the spark which ignites oppressed men.

Only through Hollywood movies is the White male power structure even remotely comfortable with female power and authority. It is perfectly okay for animals to talk, African Americans to be U.S. presidents, and for women to possess military, economic, and political power over White men, as long as it's done in the realm of fantasy and entertainment. When women refuse to be used as puppets and entertainment, the patriarchal power structure becomes fearful, paranoid, and violent. Assertive women are targeted for frustration and demoralization. Rosa Parks (Montgomery bus boycott), Lani Guinier (President Clinton appointee for Assistant Attorney General for Civil Rights), and Bari-Ellen Roberts (Texaco) are examples of women who possess a spirit that rebels against White male supremacy sabotage and oppression. Each of these women stood their ground, and they were targeted for frustration and demoralization.

The spirit of a woman absolutely defies the tyranny of oppression. Congresswoman Maxine Waters challenged the entire U. S. Government concerning its alleged role in the cocaine conspiracy, thus defying the tyranny of White male oppression! Marian Wright Edelman repeatedly hacks at what little conscience the power structure has, reminding them that *we know what they're doing to the children*! If such defiance did not exist, patriarchal White male supremacy would function much more efficiently. The revolutionary spirit of women has a strong motivational affect on their men. Never do men fight as fiercely as when fighting to protect their women. The powerlessness of women is merely a myth. The myth-makers heavily rely on this form of trickery. Women, however, will not be deceived. A spirit-filled assertiveness on the part of women will be the fuel that drives one of the world's most powerful anti-oppression movements.

CHAPTER 4

EDUCATED TO BECOME A WHITE MAN

"The true aim of female education should be, not a development of one or two, but all the faculties of the human soul, because no perfect womanhood is developed by imperfect culture."

Frances W. Harper's *The Two Offers*

Educational institutions (kindergarten through college) play *the* major role in oppressing women. Beginning in kindergarten, young girls are taught and encouraged to be obedient. Girls are frowned upon if they exhibit assertive or mildly aggressive behaviors; similar behaviors in boys are condoned and even encouraged. While this may seem cute and ladylike, it is essentially grooming the young girl to become a submissive, docile woman. Furthermore, girls are exposed to a curriculum that negates their significance to society.

> We wanted to see how well the newer books were working, so during the spring of 1992 we visited sixteen fourth-, fifth-, and sixth-grade classes in Maryland, Virginia, and Washington, D.C., and gave students this assignment: In the next five minutes write down the names of as many famous women and men as you can. They can come from anywhere in the world and they can be alive or dead, but they must be real people. . . they can't be entertainers or athletes. See if you can name at least ten men and ten women. . . . after about three minutes most run out of names. On average, students generate eleven male names but only three women's. . . . the female names generate far greater student creativity. . . Mrs. Fields, Aunt Jemima, Sarah Lee, Princess Di, . . .[1]

Such a lopsided curriculum can instill into young girls the belief that to be worthwhile is to be male—White male. And, of course, it's astronomically worse for African American girls (note that one of the women listed in the above quote was the degrading, racist stereotype of African American women—Aunt Jemima). Women who develop assertive behaviors and become educated are co-opted by the White male power structure to be used solely in the interests of the patriarchal White power structure.

Women compose the majority of students at colleges and universities. Unfortunately, the goal of education under patriarchal White rule is the continuation and growth of the racist status quo. The educational system is programmed to place White men into positions of power in society. It matters not that women make up the majority of university students; the spirit, philosophy, process, and *anticipated rewards* (high paying jobs, social status) hoped for after completion of this educational process are all controlled by patriarchal Whites. This educational process can transform women into Frankensteins (possessing someone else's brain).

From the Founding Fathers to modern corporate and political power holders, White men have set the standards and established the values that determine the kinds of goals we set and the procedures we must follow to obtain these goals. In truth, every American is born into a culture based on White male normative behavior. Since education is an integral facet of the socialization process, it is logical to state that all of us are educated to serve White men. The impact of such growth inhibiting miseducation cannot be underscored enough.

The early American reality of only White male landowners receiving an education has legally ended, but its spirit, intent, and philosophy are inherent in today's educational system/policies. Women must know this. The unspoken but effectively communicated message is that everyone can receive an education, but only White males will be the holders of power. Every tenet of education is molded and implemented in a way that keeps them well within the comfort zone and control of White men. Racial and gender unfairness is clearly within the comfort zone of patriarchal White male power. The process of being educated to become a White man does not have as its objective the placing of women into positions of power.

> Customs of education and training keep women "ghettoized" in low-paying sex-stereotyped jobs. They hold 80 percent of clerical jobs, 78 percent of service jobs, and 43 percent of professional jobs (mostly teachers and nurses). Even professional jobs, if they are "women's work," pay less than do men's lower skilled work, and often women are paid less for the same professional job. In April 1983, 69.5 percent of all women worked, but three out of five made less than $10,000 and one in three less than $7,000.[2]

The doors White men open to White women are basically assistant oppressorships which allow White male powerholders to have their agendas carried out in a manner that appears open and just. Just as with African Americans and other nonwhites, White females are mostly given positions of *authority*—not positions of *power*. Many well educated, highly intelligent, and gifted White women are often used by White male power holders to place economic and political barriers in the life paths of women and men of color. Such assistant oppressors believe that they are doing the right thing. They have "arrived."

In truth, what is termed having "arrived" actually means that the assistant oppressor woman feels that she has reached the apex of White maleness; she has psychologically become a White man. The assistant oppressor has been consumed by a lifetime of social conditioning designed to transform her into a White male. Her womanhood has been compromised and suppressed. Doing the right thing really means doing the White male thing.

The African American professional woman must be doubly careful not to become a White man. Since she and her people are members of the oppressed group, she will become an object of scorn to her people and a fool in the eyes of the White male power structure—an African American female assistant oppressor! She must fight the self-destructive White male socializing mechanism every step of the way; her sense of Africanness and womanhood demands this. Living under the image of Barbie doll, Snow White, Cinderella, and other Caucasian images of beauty is hard enough for the African woman, but to be subconsciously conditioned to become a White man adds insult to injury.

At the apex of White male based cultural-social conditioning is death of self for women. "Who am I?" cannot be answered until women define themselves according to a natural process that is free from the powerful patriarchal White male supremacist doctrine that espouses control, exploitation, and oppression of women and nonwhites. The fact that America's educational system is the vehicle for transporting Americans to the "American Dream," that fervently sought after place of high income and social status, makes it necessary for women to become drivers of this vehicle. As long as women allow the White male supremacy structure to "drive," women will be driven only to the places White males have designated for them. To achieve **kujichagulia** (self-determination), women must jump out of the patriarchal White male supremacist's vehicle and into their own. Before concluding this section, it is important that we explore the effects of female-male relationships.

The Western belief that men should control and not exhibit their emotions is a major element in the White male supremacist socializing system. According to this value system, aggressive, violent, and lustful emotions are okay for men to express. Men are rough, rugged, and tough; they growl, bark, yell, and hit hard. All of this fits hand-in-glove with the survival-of-the-ruthless mentality that is inherent under White male supremacy. Girls are socialized within this context. Girls become women within this context. Women seek self-actualization within this context.

Understand and remember: Under White male supremacy, "girls will be girls" and "boys will be boys" really means that girls are reared to become entertainers of men. Men rule, work hard, growl, and snarl while women entertain them between the acts of ruling, working, barking, growling, and snarling. It is within such a pathological context that we come to understand the effect of White male supremacist socialization on female-male relationships.

A woman socialized to be a man cannot have a successful wife-husband relationship with a man. Her socialization has been perverted. If she submits to a less than human, entertainment role, the so-called relationship will be "successful." If she has become an assistant oppressor (which is a combination of fake White man and flunky White man) her so-called relationship will be competitive, manipulative, and deceitful. Since the men have not been socialized to be honest, caring, and just, they cannot relate to women in an honest, caring, and just manner. Since she has been socialized to *imitate* White males, she is *confused* as to how to *relate* to him as a woman. The relationship is, more than likely, doomed. Once the superficial act of dating and romance ends, they both find that nothing's left but a ruthless game of mutual subjugation. Such women end up in "no man's land." They have been programmed to be and think outside of their nature. They are lost and confused, trying to figure it out and discover themselves in this White male supremacist twilight zone. Patriarchal White supremacy is anti-family, anti-justice, and anti-spirituality; very few female-male relationships can flourish or survive under White male supremacy.

CHAPTER 5

PUBLIC SCHOOL ABUSE OF NONWHITE AND POOR FEMALE PARENTS

America's educational system abuses African American, Latino, and poor women. These women experience frequent disrespect and hear outright lies from some school administrators and teachers. Even worse, African American, Latino, and poor women are the educational system's scapegoats used to camouflage genocidal, racist policies and practices. This exists because patriarchal White supremacists know the necessity of dividing, frustrating, and conquering the children, parents, and communities of nonwhite people. Since children are mandated by law to attend school, the patriarchal power structure delights in having what amounts to mandated guinea pigs for their miseducational laboratories. It is quite common for inner city elementary, middle, and high schools, which are generally majority African American and/or Latino, to have a large number of children on psychostimulants such as Ritalin, Adderall, Desoxyn, and Cylert. It is equally common to find huge numbers of African American and poor children, especially African American boys, placed in alternative schools. Alternative to what? The alternative to an educational setting designed to create thinkers, physicians, pilots, entrepreneurs, and the like. Most alternative schools are created to assure the comfort and "safety" of White children, teachers, and administrators.

It is through bogus Individualized Educational Program meetings and placement meetings that these children of the oppressed end up on medication, placed in special education classes, and placed into alternative schools.

Through the use of titles and professional jargon, the parents (mostly single mothers or grandmothers) are deceived by the pretense of caring (i.e., "Jamal is such a darling, we all really love him and we know that placing him on Ritalin and placing him in the special class will really afford him the least restrictive and beneficial learning environment"). They consent to place their children into educational concentration camps (alternative schools), Behavior Disorder classes (in-house laboratories), and put on psychostimulants (preparing the child to become an addict). A vast number of these children will end up dropping out of school, hanging out in neighborhood parks or on street corners. Many of the special education teachers and school social workers entice these economically depressed, socially oppressed mothers into putting their children on Social Security Disability; the mother is then able to receive a monthly check. This diabolical act assures that the child will be permanently dependent and simply messed up. Every element of the patriarchal White supremacist power structure makes money off of African American destruction. Destroying the lives of their adult victims' children is indeed the most demonic act of the patriarchal White supremacist power structure.

The children's mothers and grandmothers are awed and intimidated and often feel that they are helpless against such a system, and will sometimes blame themselves for the problems plaguing their young; the oppressed sometimes blame themselves for causing their oppression in the same manner that many physically abused children and women blame themselves for causing the abuse. Such logic allows the true perpetrator to hide his blood-stained hands.

Many school teachers and administrators view African American, Latino, and poor women as inferior. These parents are quite often the topic of teacher lounge conversations. These teachers, most of whom are White females, degrade the very people that provide them with their middle-class incomes. Most of the time, African American, Latino, and poor mothers are judged, as are their children, before the teachers and school administrators even meet them. As a result, every interaction with these women and their children is similar to master-slave interactions. Financial resources for learning technology are not sought for these youth; teachers are generally impatient with these children and their parents; the boys become candidates for labels, special education placement, and medication; the parents are deliberately misinformed; and the curriculum does nothing to empower the students, parents, and community. It is by design that the school's curriculum is not supported by top-of-the-line textbooks, advanced classes, vocational classes for students not planning to attend college, or mentoring programs designed to bring positive African American/Latino male adults into these children's lives. No type of educational infrastructure is developed for the children of African American, Latino, and poor parents. The result is a community filled with hopelessness, blight, and crime—exactly what the patriarchal White power structure planned.

Tired, frustrated African American, Latino, and poor mothers and grandmothers are blamed by career oriented politicians, police chiefs, school board administrators, and others for the problems taking place in schools and communities. Many of the blamers are either ignorant or racist. The inner city schools that these children attend, on the one hand, are used as scapegoats and political footballs by power brokers who mean the children, their parents and community no good. On the other hand, these schools and the children keep many Whites in their middle-class lifestyles. These children's mothers may work several jobs. They do love their children but this is not discussed. These women are stigmatized. They are often intimidated and lied to by teachers and administrators. The teachers are often impatient with mother and child, and they are often rushed along and receive superficial attention to their concerns. When one of these oppressed mothers does challenge the system, she is thrust into a bureaucratic maze and nasty attitudes that are designed to wear her down. This assertive mother is feared and despised by the White male power structure. She may ignite a fire that would threaten White male power.

African American, Latino, and poor parents are between a rock and a hard place: They are confronted by a genocidal curriculum and hostile, unfair policies. The mothers and grandmothers of oppressed groups are, unknowingly for most, in a war: If their children are truly empowered, the patriarchal White power structure will eventually lose its power. And White male patriarchs equate losing their power to oppress others with losing their lives. All oppressed groups must understand this dynamic of White supremacy—it's either White supremacy or death. Oppressing others and breathing are synonymous to them.

Women must permanently disrupt and replace oppressor's slave-making curriculum. Policies are created to protect this curriculum and frustrate parents' attempts to save their children. Instead, miseducated youth are placed into oppressed communities, and the deadly cycle repeats. When children suffer, mothers suffer, and when mothers suffer children suffer. Those mothers and grandmothers who are assertive must assist those mothers, especially the young mothers, who need help until they are strong enough to handle situations under patriarchal White male supremacy. Women must develop empowerment/self-help networks designed to keep them and their families alive and prosperous under an unjust, racist power structure. Women must ignore policy maintaining protocols that will be thrown at them by system maintainers. Push your agenda. Do not feel pressured to fit the mode of the people employed in the oppressive system. This is a life or death struggle and must be approached as such. Public education will change in direct proportion to the degree of pressure mothers and grandmothers put on the system.

CHAPTER 6

SOCIAL WELFARE AND WOMEN

Some social service agencies are in actuality social *disservice* agencies that do little more than place women and girls into a revolving door of dehumanization. And while the public, many of whom have been deliberately miseducated about the poor, especially poor African Americans, tend to believe that African Americans are abusing tax dollars, the truth is most of this money goes to social service providers. Poor people, the majority of whom are White, (African Americans make up a disproportionate share of the poor due to our percentage of the U.S. population), receive *services,* not *money.*[1] I know from years of social services experience that many middle-class Whites, especially White women, earn their living off of poor African Americans and Latinos. Even though I have mixed feelings about welfare to work legislation, I know that the future of African American women must not be based on government care. Underpaid working women still need childcare and medical benefits.

I know several mothers hide the fact that they prepare women's hair in their homes or sell dinners at home because their case workers will take what little food stamps they are receiving. These women do not fit the White male stereotypes, and there are thousands of women in this unpleasant situation. The social services motto seems to be, "You are not allowed to become, in any degree, truly independent of this agency." White supremacist social service institutions have no intention of alleviating female poverty, especially African American and Latino female poverty.

Approximately 37 percent of all poor people live in households headed by women, and of all single-parent families 94 percent of those in poverty are headed by women. In White mother-headed households, slightly less than half the children are poor, whereas almost two-thirds of children in both African American and Latin families are poor.[2]

Social service agencies are supposed to assist families in a manner that empowers the families to be self-sufficient. However, this does not happen. Women become stuck with these agencies. Many of the agencies function in an all-or-nothing manner, meaning that the women must either stay dependent or they will be abruptly cut off from all services.

Institutional discrimination permeates American systems so deeply that we may not recognize it. Based on hostile attitudes reified in rules, regulations, and procedures, its forms—racism, sexism, ageism, . . . deny equal rights and opportunities to groups even when no individual prejudice may be involved. Moreover, types of institutional discrimination interact with each other and with classism, enforcing the status quo of our society: People discriminated against are more likely to be poor, and if more than one discrimination is present, the likelihood of poverty is even greater. For example, an aged African American woman is in triple jeopardy of being poor because of her age, race, and gender.[3]

Many women need the services temporarily, but this fact is ignored. As a result, women often have to moonlight to wean themselves from the agency. Women are damned if they do and damned if they don't. African American women, especially, are labeled from the outset as being "welfare queens." It is well known that the stereotypical picture of America's welfare recipient is that of an African American female who, according to White supremacy, becomes pregnant for the sole purpose of receiving welfare payments. I have worked with hundreds of single mothers and I have yet to meet one that fits this White supremacist profile. Again, the White patriarch's objective is to paint African American and Latino women as lazy people who simply feed off the labor of others. This allows the patriarchal White supremacist to justify his ruthless control and oppression of African Americans and Latinos, and to have other people, even African Americans and Latinos, to condone the oppression of their Brothers and Sisters.

White male patriarchal values laid the foundation for America's, and much of the world's, social welfare agencies.[4] This fact makes America's social welfare agencies social **disservice** agencies that humiliate, confuse, and frustrate many of the women that seek their help. Although many of the social welfare agency employees are women, they are mandated to implement the often callous, inhumane policies set forth by the White male supremacist power structure. These female employees are faced with the rat-race reality of "do your job or lose your job." Such a duality of pathological relations is found at every level of the social welfare system. The female client and the female employee are both victims of a process controlled by White male patriarchy.

The dynamic of humiliation is in place before the mother walks through the agency's door. Since dependency is viewed as an evil and rugged individualism a virtue, these dependent women are set up to fail. The White male power structure is not altruistic; it is really sadistic in that it delights in socially and economically abusing, exploiting, stigmatizing, and crippling its female victims under the guise of helping them.

Females, whether elderly or teenage, must bare their souls and give up much of their privacy if they want to receive social welfare services—services that are grudgingly given. Sitting in agency lobbies like cattle waiting to be branded, women take turns going into social workers' offices to be given an often intimidating verbal drill on the do's and don'ts of receiving various welfare services, such as food debit cards and public housing. If these women seek full-time employment, they know their services will probably be canceled. Seldom are they allowed an opportunity to get on their feet before dropping welfare services. Their choice is simple: remain dependent or suffer. The sadistic nature of patriarchal White male power is clearly manifested.

Women living in government subsidized housing are strongly discouraged from developing relationships with men. As if the stereotype of being sexually promiscuous isn't enough, women who are involved with social welfare agencies are told that men are not allowed to stay in the dwelling any more than two or three days. Only people who believe the patriarchal stereotypes fail to see below the surface. Both men and women seeking to establish relationships are oppressed by the White male power structure. Thus, men and women should combine their resources because the White male supremacist structure will not support the formation of families. Men and women must work together, for they will get no help from the "do gooders."

Policies. Social welfare policies embody the values, attitudes, and agenda of the patriarchal White male rulers of America. Rhetoric such as "pull yourself up by your bootstraps" and "father knows best" masks the fear, paranoia, and ruthfulness of White men who view women and nonwhites as enemies. This nation's universities and schools of social work and sociology also function from this toxic foundation. Professors, many unknowingly, are simply instructing students on how to maintain a social welfare system that socially, psychologically, and emotionally mutilates women, especially African American and Latino women. Amos N. Wilson stated that America's educational system is designed to train students to become servants.[5] What women must understand is that they are being trained to help a patriarchal White male supremacist system subjugate women. The textbook companies, universities, and social welfare agencies are each controlled by the patriarchal White male power structure. Entirely new and humane social service constructs and systems must be developed. The sabotage of women is a deliberate plan which feeds the pathological egos of patriarchal White male rulers. There is a tremendous sense of accomplishment and ego building experienced by White men when they view evening news programs showing welfare recipients receiving government cheese or simply giving thanks for the crumbs they receive. The entire social service/welfare system is sadistic and must not be viewed as a potential or actual source of help for African American and Latino women.

CHAPTER 7

RELIGION, *MEN*-ISTERS, AND WOMEN

What is "religion" under patriarchal White male supremacy? I remember listening to a speech by Dr. John Henrik Clarke, in which he stated that in their attempt to understand African spirituality, Europeans and Western Asians chopped it up and placed it into categories which they called "religion." Dr. Clarke stated that spirituality is a way of life that cannot be compartmentalized.

In her book *Yurugu: An African-Centered Critique of European Cultural Thought and Behavior*, author Marimba Ani, states:

> If one looks for a sense of the supernatural, the sacred, or extraordinary in European culture, undoubtedly the only area of experience that approaches the "religious" in this sense is that of "science." It is only what is considered to be science and scientific method that is regarded with the awe and humility that in other cultures represents the "religious attitude."[1]

Out of touch. The White supremacist power structure is out of touch with the spirit of Truth, Justice, and Righteousness (ancient African principles of Maat). If it can't be quantified and placed into neat categories, then rationalized to fit their almost robotic thought processes, then it is primitive, pagan, and unchristian. Since White supremacy's social/cultural structure and philosophy are pathologically corrupt, racist, and sexist, what can you expect of its religious philosophies and practices? Marimba Ani states that, "The relationship of European religion to other aspects of the culture is symptomatic of a persistent despiritualization and desacralization of experience and can be shown to be a characteristic of "Westerness" since its archaic stages."[2] Simply put, pathology spreads in the same manner as does other diseases. Since the core ideologies are racist and sexist, they spread to all other ideologies—especially religious ideologies. Women, in their fight for self-determination, are in many ways fighting androids, not humans. An android can only function in a numerical context, not in the human realm of feelings and spirituality. They simply think differently. Again, quoting Marimba Ani:

> This mode of thought that has worked so well to produce the kind of technical and social order that Europeans desire has also created a moral and spiritual disaster. The formal religious statement has taken on the form of the rational state and has left Europeans no access to the necessarily spiritual reservoirs of human morality.[3]

How do you fight someone whose religious system is spiritually and morally void? What is the designated role of women within such a religious system? First, women must not waste their time trying to appeal to the nonexisting moral nature of the patriarchal White supremacist power structure. White men in positions of power know their actions are unjust; bringing what they already know to their attention is a waste of time because the power structure's goal is to *keep power by any means*. Second, women have, generally, been designated by the male dominated religious structure as witches and purveyors of sin. Women are, from childhood, taught that they are religiously inferior to men. Marimba Ani states that, "The patriarchal nature of early Indo-European religion indicates more than a desire of men to dominate women. It also results from the association of "maleness" with superiority and "femaleness" with inferiority."[4]

If a woman believes she is less than a man instead of different and equal, she has set herself up for varied types of abuse. Organized religion is sometimes abusive of women because it lacks spirituality. Spirituality teaches the person that the normal and most productive way to conduct one's life is the spiritual way. Spirituality and equality go hand-in-hand. The spiritual person does not see her/himself as superior to anyone; such thinking is not normal and makes no sense. Within spirituality, different only means different. Men and women are different and equal. Their natures are complementary. They live because the other lives and die when the other dies. Let us now look into the often bizarre relationship between religion, *men*-isters, and women.

Several years ago, during a group discussion, a woman stated that females menstruate because they sinned in the Garden of Eden, and God punished them by making them bleed once a month. Such falsehoods were not created by women. This is a theology created by men for women. During ancient history, Indo-European men fashioned an angry God who subjugates women.[5] As stated earlier in **Patriarchy and Female Subjugation**, Africans worshipped goddesses and gods before the advent of Judaism, Christianity, and Islam. In general, if women desire fair treatment from religious institutions, they must rebel and challenge the religious patriarchal status quo, which is exactly what AME Bishop Vashti McKenzie did, and rightfully won. My minister and many other African American Baptist male ministers don't believe that women should pastor churches. God works through women as much as God does through men. If women were inferior,

God would have given men wombs—and the ability to impregnate themselves and give birth. If this sounds ridiculous then my point is made. It is amazing how a person could be so "religious" but so blind and judgemental of the people (females) who make up the majority of the congregation and provide most of the tithes. Women should not wait on the kindness of men who have been socialized to believe God has placed women in a lowly position. Now let's look at the structure of most churches in America.

The *men*-ister. Although many church congregations are overwhelmingly female, men are at the head. There's nothing wrong with men being *ministers*, but there is something wrong with the imbalance in the number of female and male ministers. More women should be at the head of churches. Women must not imitate men in power. Positive change, not imitation, is the goal. Many churches are run using female dollars, a percentage of which goes to pay the salary of the man who tells the females what God has told him. I guess God doesn't speak directly to women. In some churches women treat the *men*-ister as if he is God; it is in this type of church where women are likely to be pimped by their *men*-ister.

Women who view their femininity as a curse are more than willing to believe, follow, and obey *men*-isters. Some of these women believe it is a sin for women to become ministers. Once a woman begins to believe that she has been condemned by the creator to a lowly condition in life, she will cease all attempts to become self-actualized and self-determined. The spiritual well-being of a woman is in jeopardy when such madness exists.

Since the ministry is becoming a business where big salaries are given to those who are the most charismatic in delivering their view of God's Word, women will

face great competition in their attempts to become ministers. Again, women must refrain from imitating the con
artist, the smoke-and-mirrors tactics of some *men*-isters.
Holding the position of minister must be based on Truth,
Justice, and Righteousness (Maat). That which has been
lost in the *men*-istry can be regained by women ministers
advocating for a spiritual lifestyle instead of empty proc-
lamations. In this practice and in the act of rebelling against
White male supremacy, women can save the world.

PART FOUR

THE WICKED, THE MAD, AND THE SPIRITUAL

CHAPTER 1

THE NECESSITY OF FEMALE REBELLION

The law cannot do it for us. *We must do it for ourselves.*
Women in this country must become revolutionaries.
Shirley Chisholm

Women must culturally, economically, educationally, spiritually, and politically rebel against the patriarchal White male power structure. The Black woman must
rebel for the sake of the Black nation. The White woman
must rebel in order to end her velvet chains of slavery
and prostitution. Other women must rebel for a combination of all the above. If you want to be free you must
rebel. If morally, mentally sound families are to become
the norm, then women must rebel against the ruthless,
immoral, wickedly clever White male supremacist power
structure. Women, in general, can learn what not to do
in their struggle for self-determination from African
Americans. bell hooks' comments are both enlightening
and sobering:

> Revolutionary black liberation struggle in the United
> States was undermined by outmoded patriarchal em-
> phasis on nationhood and masculine rule, the absence
> of a strategy for coalition building that would keep a
> place for non-black allies in struggle, and the lack of
> sustained programs for education for critical conscious-
> ness that would continually engage black folks of all
> classes in a process of radical politicization.[1]

Ms. hooks' concern about "the lack of sustained programs for education for critical consciousness..."[2] deserves careful analysis, comprehension, and systematic implementation. Women must reach, teach, recruit, and retain other women and men. Consciousness raising education is the glue that will link all four elements. Much of the patriarchal White male power structure's success is due to its use of education, and sometimes miseducation. Women must read literature to strengthen their quest for self-determination.

It is significant that women's goals are the checkmating of the patriarchal White male power structure. Women must *not* believe that men of color, especially African American and Native American men, are the enemy. Remember: For the most part, these men, no matter what positions of authority some may hold, are either puppets or cheap imitators of the White male supremacists. Also, women must not have as their goal the imitation of the White male power structure. Freedom is not obtained through imitation of one's oppressor. *The goal must not be to become White men.*

Black women must have included in their revolutionary goal the mental and spiritual freedom of themselves, their children, their men, and their communities. They must view their people as a tribe. Africans/African Americans must view themselves as a tribe because this creates a unified front. Africans have been the numero uno victims of White supremacy. Whether medical doctor or street corner hustler, Africans are in the same boat.

White women must be very careful not to become imitators of their men. If White women try to imitate White males in power, they will not gain true freedom; they will remain enslaved by the doctrine of patriarchal White male supremacy, and in the final analysis will become just as ruthless as men. White women must seek to develop the humanity of the White race. This is the charge placed upon the White women who rebel against the White male power structure.

Women from the various countries in Asia, South America, and the Pacific basin must, like the African American/African woman, seek to free themselves, their men, and their children from the mental and spiritual slavery of the White supremacist structure. Although these groups generally exhibit more tribal behavior than African Americans, they are sometimes enthusiastic imitators of Whites. As is expected, the victims of White supremacy will experience a substantial degree of ambivalence about culturally, economically, educationally, politically, and spiritually rebelling against their oppressor. Many victims have developed a love-hate relationship with the White power structure. And, as sick as it seems, some victims have learned to *enjoy* the abuse and subjugation they receive. An intrapersonal warfare is taking place in the hearts and minds of White supremacy's victims, especially its victims of color. Like the enslaved African who was afraid to leave the plantation after emancipation because he/she did not know how to survive without "massa," today's victims may not be able to conceive of a life without the present day White male supremacist "massa."

Under oppression, rebellion must become synonymous with womanhood. Women must rebel in order to become women. A pathological White male power structure has no right whatsoever directing the course of female development. Business as usual must be challenged

and changed if the chains of mental and spiritual slavery
are to be broken.

CHAPTER 2

RECOMMENDATIONS

Women are fighting to obtain self-determination against a patriarchal White power structure that is nonspiritual, aggressive, competitive, paranoid, guiltless, and extremely cunning. Have no illusions.

What the Sisters Have to Say

A quote from the 25th Supreme Basileus, Norma Soloman White, of the oldest Greek-letter organization established by African American college women, Alpha Kappa Alpha, sums up the mission of AKA Sorority, Inc.: "Sorors, the first biennial of this administration is history. We move on then to the next two years fully aware that we have many of miles to go before we sleep, lots of coats to give to the homeless and needy, hundreds of at risk children to keep 'On Track,' thousands of lives to save through the 'Buckle Up' Program, millions of voters to get to the polls in November, hundreds of Sorors to bring home, many letters to write to legislatures, added steps to take to state capitols, additional schools to build in Africa, numerous black businesses and black families to support and more bodies to keep healthy."[1]

The Sisters of Delta Sigma Theta Sorority, Inc. are also on point in their tireless effort to reach, help, teach, and elevate their African/African American Sisters and Brothers. Exhibiting the social awareness and courage that exemplify Delta Sigma Theta Sorority, the Deltas established The Delta Academy to save young girls. The academies have a cultural-educational mission designed to develop dynamic, progressive African American female leadership. Deltas have also implemented the Summit V campaign designed to help recognize, treat, and decrease the incidences of clinical depression among African American women. Moving across the Atlantic to the Motherland, Delta Sigma Theta continues to provide financial support for the Thika Memorial Hospital, located in Nairobi, Kenya. The Deltas initially funded a maternity and health services wing at the hospital in 1955.[2] Clearly, the Deltas are on point.

Nothing but continuous praise must go to The National Black Women's Health Project, whose mission is "to improve the health of Black women by providing wellness education and services, self-help group development, health information, and advocacy."[3] Their headquarters is located at 600 Pennsylvania Ave., SE, Suite 310, Washington, DC 20003. Their programs and services include: Self-Help and Chapter Development, Walking for Wellness, Substance Abuse Prevention Program, National Conference, and Annual Self-Help Developers Meeting/ Leadership Development Institute. Their publications consist of: *Vital Signs News Magazine* (published annually) and *Sister Link* (quarterly newsletter). Videos include *On Becoming a Woman: Mothers and Daughters Talking Together; It's OK to Peek; Our Bodies, Our Voices, Our Choices: A Black Women's Primer On Reproductive Health & Rights*, 1998; and *Body and Soul: The Black Women's Guide to Physical Health and Emotional Well-Being*, edited by Linda Villarosa.[4]

No discussion on the survival of African American people would even be remotely complete without mentioning the theories of psychiatrist Frances Cress Welsing, a bold and dynamic Sister. Dr. Welsing states that the problem facing people of color, especially Black people, is White supremacy, which is based in the global White community's fear of genetic annihilation by people of color. Dr. Welsing states that the nine areas of human activity—economics, education, entertainment, labor, law, politics, religion, sex, and war are all dominated by White supremacist beliefs and practices.[5] African American women must study Dr. Welsing's theory and then develop a different way of believing and acting.

This next set of recommendations stated here is by no means absolute or perfect and should be cross-referenced, altered, and even erased by women according to their needs. The recommendations are written in, hopefully, concise detail.

Issue Focused

Women must unite around common problems. This helps to keep unity within the ranks, so to speak. This prevents women from being divided and conquered by the strategies and ploys that will certainly be placed in their path. White women must not ignore or downplay issues that negatively effect African Americans and Latino women. The White male power structure expects White women to become or remain loyal to it. Each woman must take the other's situation as if it were her own. A threat to one is a threat to all. I must honestly state here that the approach used to gain self-determination must not be European-centered. That which is European-centered is rooted in "The patriarchal nature of early Indo-European religion."[6] Marimba Ani states:

> In our analysis male domination has a specific history in European culture and is linked to the other cultural forms in a uniquely "European" manner. This phenomenon should not be understood as a universal, because while it may have similar appearances in different cultures, the degree of intensity varies as does the relationship to the *asili* of the culture.[7]

Marimba Ani is explaining that "separation, oppo-sition, and dominance" are inherent within European think-ing/culture.[8] Therefore, to use a European model is to do and receive more of the same.

Health

Herbal and holistic medicine soon took their place in my overall approach. I learned that nontraditional medi-cine and nutrition had a healthy place alongside tradi-tional modern approaches. I also began to exercise. I discovered that exercise improved my energy level and increased weight loss. The more regularly I exercised, the better I felt.[9]

It is vital that women eat healthy and exercise. Tak-ing a multivitamin-mineral supplement is a wonderful con-tribution to excellent health. Also, look into natural herbal supplements such as Goldenseal and Echinacea. There must be consistent monitoring of the foods eaten. Don't over do fried, greasy, sugar laden, starchy foods. African Ameri-can women must be especially careful of their diet because of the high obesity-related high blood pressure rates for African Americans. Don't smoke. Don't drink alcohol or only drink in moderation. Unleash the will power that will help you to change your eating habits and that will help you to develop and stick to an exercise regimen. Women can't fight patriarchal White supremacy from hospital beds.

Non-Anti-Male

Women's organizations must not become anti-male. This clouds and seriously confuses the issues. Nonwhite men do not run the world—White men run the world. White nations are the only ones that have the military and economic might to directly or indirectly determine the destiny of other nations. Although some nonwhite men imitate White men, women must remember that these men are just that—imitators of White men! African American and Latino men, for example, must not be viewed as the culprits of female oppression. These men have been miseducated by the patriarchal White male power structure, and will foolishly take on their oppressor's views of women.

The true culprit, of course, is the patriarchal White power structure. It is this power structure which has, for the last 500 years, set up a social-economic-political system that oppresses women and people of color. Its political, religious, economic, military, business, and even medical leaders have, by way of practices and policies, mandated the oppression of women. So, women must not become anti-male, but anti-patriarchal White power structure.

No Imitation

Again, women must not imitate the pathological behavior of the White male power structure. Such behavior is self-destructive. Would you imitate a suicidal person? As women move into positions of power, they must seek to change the "good ol' boys" structure. These women must seek to change or eliminate institutional policies and practices that deny opportunity to women and nonwhites. These women will be repeatedly attacked by their White male "peers" and female assistant oppressors, but must remain steadfast in challenging and changing the oppressive power structure.

Voting

All politicians need the votes of women. Women must register to vote and must vote in record numbers. Voting reveals that serious divisions among women can occur. Women living in $200,000 a year households may be philosophically detached from women living in $25,000 a year households. Women who are sincere in their efforts to help all women, regardless of income level or race, will have no trouble here. But, those women who view themselves as outside of women's issues due to their financial status will serve, either directly or indirectly, the interests of the White male power structure. All women should vote in a strategic, focused, well organized manner with clear objectives and in record numbers. It is also crucial that women in each state find out what is required to reinstitute voting privileges to women who are taken off probation; with thousands of African American women in America's prisons it is easy to see how important reinstituting voting privileges has become.

Women must also run for political offices in record numbers. Women should be represented at every level of government and must, for example, possess the fighter's spirit of Maxine Waters of California. Women must *believe* that this should be done and that women deserve a significantly larger share of *power*. Single mothers should run for political office. Hispanic women should run for political office. Physically challenged women should run for political office. Native American women should run for political office. Women should finance women's political campaigns (this would prevent being purchased by wealthy White men). Women should *never* limit themselves to only certain types (those perceived as acceptable to White men) running for political offices. Change means just that—CHANGE!

Prison

Prisons in America are the new slave plantations. With more than 90,000 women incarcerated, and African American women constituting the majority, it becomes clear that African Americans, Latinos, Native Americans, and poor Whites are targeted to be the new slaves. Women are forced to aggressively confront the political-social-economic-racist causes behind the imprisonment of their sisters and men. No rehabilitation takes place in America's prisons; slaves were never taught how to escape from the plantation. White male supremacy has rendered these imprisoned women useless except for use as slaves on their prison plantations. Mothers, daughters, and wives are the modern-day field hands in America's so-called criminal injustice system. Remember, when women suffer their children also suffer. Instead of trying to change the prisons, women will benefit more from aggressively attacking the social-economic causes behind female incarceration.

Media

The ownership and control of print and electronic media by patriarchal White male supremacists, besides their control of the educational system, are very dangerous for women. bell hooks does a brilliant job of discussing this in her book *Black Looks: Race and Representation*. It is through their media that White men teach, encourage, and condone the abuse of women. They use their print and electronic media to mold women into what they want women to be, and to program others to believe that they have a God-given right to subjugate females. Women are at once abused and prostituted by the patriarchal White media. Since many people's minds have been numbed by the media, they are unable to see the pathological, sadistic nature of the media. Women must boldly confront and change the nature of the media's insidious practices. Letter writing/faxing/e-mailing and picketing campaigns can go a long way toward bringing about positive change.

AIDS

Women, especially African/African American women, must launch a no-compromise campaign aimed at stopping the spread of AIDS. The true cause of AIDS— White genetic survival—must be made known; the psychological pain experienced by all African people must be addressed; and the habit of too many African/African Americans living a destructive lifestyle must be confronted and prevented. Grassroots campaigns that target Brothers and Sisters must be developed and delivered in night clubs, gyms, community centers, churches, parks, and businesses located in the community. We must go to the various places that our people frequent. A part of the AIDS prevention grassroots campaign must also focus on condemning media and artists that encourage the living of destructive lifestyles through their medium and their art. One strategy that I use in attracting teens and pre-teens is advertising that lunch/snacks will be served *after* the workshop/ activity/program. Ask night club owners to allow you seven minutes to make a presentation (don't forget to leave information fliers). Be creative, consistent, and bold in reaching/teaching the people. Utilize radio talk programs (which are free) to reach the people. Hold press conferences designed to highlight the life and death significance of the issue. Demand that state and federal elected officials address the sexual madness occurring among men in this nation's prisons. The male prisons are becoming HIV breeding grounds. Advocate for Sisters to have their boyfriends and husbands tested upon exiting prisons.

Your Men

The men of oppressed women are themselves oppressed, especially African American, Native American, and Latino men. If, due to White supremacist miseducation, your men exhibit self-destructive behaviors and ideas, you should confront them. Your men must be reeducated; demand that your men develop and consistently implement African-centered rites of passage programs designed to systematically develop African manhood. When oppressed men and women fight each other only their oppressor wins. Miseducation is necessary for dividing and conquering a people. In the spirit of love, demand that your men treat you as an equal. Let him know that he's not less of a man because he treats you as an equal. Let your men know that you do not want them basing their manhood on the oppressor's definition. In a loving, respectful manner demand excellence from your men. Spiritually and philosophically unified women and men are an unmovable force. Such a team would not be oppressed very long.

Maat

Maat is the ancient African concept/goddess of Truth, Justice, and Righteousness. To be successful in challenging patriarchal White male supremacy, women must function in the spirit of Maat. Only an aggressive, unified approach governed by the principles of Maat can checkmate the deceitful, unjust, immoral practices of the patriarchal White male power structure.

Business Ownership

Allow me to again quote Marimba Ani before stating my beliefs relating to women's business ownership:

Women, please do not place money before God, Jehovah, Ra, Allah, the Creator. Don't imitate the non-spiri-

Because of the spiritual void in European culture and its ideological individualism, capitalism was able to gain hold and to flourish; in turn it supported these themes. And because of the success of capitalism in the West the concepts of individual freedom and possession were reinforced, while any attempt to discover human spirituality was discouraged.[10]

tual, ruthless behavior of White men. Women must own and operate mom and pop stores, computer businesses, income tax businesses, dry cleaners, automotive repair businesses, photography studios, pharmacies, clothing stores, investment companies, and any other business that come to mind. Business owners have a certain degree of political and social clout. Business owners play a crucial role in the nation's Gross National Product. With the nature and availability of work permanently changing, it is wise for women to seek business ownership as a means of family survival. It is not good for women to primarily hold the consumer role in society. Many families have only the mother as the sole provider; these mothers, especially, must be creative and aggressive in starting either full-or part-time businesses. Business ownership must never again be mainly perceived as a male-only venture.

One event which Sisters and Brothers conducted in various U.S. cities was recycling Black Dollars Tours. Women, especially African American women, should start these tours and focus primarily on businesses owned by African American women. Be creative and bold in this endeavor. Go on community based talk radio programs (which are free) to explain and discuss your business. Ask ministers for three minutes to explain your business during church service. Since many African American businesses possess little advertising capital, it is important to use grass-roots guerilla marketing techniques. Continue these techniques even after you have acquired enough money to buy regular types of advertising. The forming of business networks that center on group buying can also be of tremendous benefit to African American women businesses, especially hair/skin/nail care. Long-term goals should focus on owning wholesale and manufacturing businesses. Difficult? Yes. Impossible? No. Necessary? Absolutely!

Sexual and Physical Abuse

Women must do whatever is necessary to stop and prevent physical and sexual abuse of themselves and their daughters. This includes physical self defense, advocating for stiffer laws that penalize abusers and molesters of women and children, and educating women on how fear prevents them from taking action. If a man knows he is likely to pay one hell of a price for abusing and molesting a woman or girl, he is less likely to make an attempt. Stopping sexual and physical abuse is a do or die situation which requires very little theorizing and a great deal of forceful, direct action.

In closing, I recommend the following:

- Every morning, look in the mirror and say, I am God's child. I am fearfully and wonderfully made, every hair has been numbered, and no one has my finger prints. I am a Proverbs 31 woman.
- I deserve the best husband and will not settle for anything less.
- My children will always respect me.
- I will teach my daughter how to be beautiful, respected, and admired, like her mother.
- I will teach my son to respect women and not be a mama's boy. My son will never participate in a "train," rape, or abuse a woman.
- I will teach my husband not be sexist in a culture that devalues women.
- I will not gossip about my sisters, but will encourage them to be all they can become.
- I will call, write, and /or e-mail any institution that does not reflect the best in African American women.
- I will organize other women on my block, in my children's school, in my church, and on my job to resist racism and sexism. Let's get busy!

ENDNOTES

Part One: Cause, Effect, and Madness

When Love Hurts: Spouse Abuse and Sexual Molestation

1. Heart & Soul. August/September 2000. Page 78. *Behind Closed Doors {living a life of abuse}* by Pamela Newkirk and Rhonda B. Graham.

2. Ibid.

Bitch, Hoe, or Queen? The Role of Women in Rap Music and Videos

1. Latifah, Q. *Ladies First: Revelations of a Strong Woman.* William Morrow and Company, Inc. New York, NY. 1999.

2. Ibid.

SBF

1. Essence. May 1987. Page 32. *A Conversation With Dr. Frances Cress Welsing.*

AIDS and African/African American Women

1. HIV InSite AIDS Epidemic Update. December 1999. http://hivinsite.ucsf.edu/social/un/2098.44d3.html

2. Ibid.

3. Ibid.

4. HIV InSite. March 16, 1998. http://hivinsite.usaf.edu

5. Ibid.

6. Ibid.

7. Cress Welsing, F. *The Isis Papers: The Keys to the Colors.* Third World Press. Chicago, Illinois. 1991.

8. Ibid.

9. Ibid.

10. Cookson, J. and Nottingham, J. *A Survey of Chemical and Biological Warfare.* 1969.

White Male Supremacy

1. hooks, b. *Killing Rage: Ending Racism.* Henry Holt & Company, Inc. New York, NY. 1995.

2. Ibid.

3. Cress Welsing, F. *The Isis Papers: The Keys to the Colors.* Third World Press. Chicago, Illinois. 1991.

4. Davis, A. Y. *Women Race & Class.* Random House. New York, NY. 1983.

5. Ibid.

6. Keppel, R. D., Birnes, W. J. *Signature Killers: Interpreting the Calling Cards of the Serial Murderer.* Pocket Books. New York, New York. 1997.

7. Bradley, M. *The IceMan Inheritance: Prehistoric Sources of Western Man's Racism, Sexism and Aggression.* Kayode Publications. 1991.

The Myth of White Normalcy

1. Seldes, G. *The Great Thoughts.* Ballantine Books. New York, NY. 1985.

2. Ani, M. *Yurugu: An African-Centered Critique of European Cultural Thought and Behavior.* Africa World Press, Inc. Trenton, NJ. 1994.

3. Ibid.

4. Ibid.

5. Ibid.

6. Ibid.

7. Ibid.

8. Willinsky, J. *Learning to Divide the World: Education at Empire's End.* University of Minnesota Press. Minneapolis, MN. 1998.

9. Ibid.

10. Ani, M. *Yurugu: An African-Centered Critique of European Cultural Thought and Behavior.* Africa World Press, Inc. Trenton, NJ. 1994.

Patriarchy and Female Subjugation

1. hooks, b. *Killing Rage: Ending Racism.* Henry Holt & Company, Inc. New York, NY. 1995.

2. Ibid.

3. Diop, C. A. *The African Origin of Civilization Myth or Reality.* Lawrence Hill Books. Chicago, Illinois. 1983.

4. Ibid.

5. Ibid.

Part Two: The Women

African American Women: The Crucifixion of Mother

1. hooks, b. *Black Looks: Race and Representation.* South End Press. Boston, MA. 1992.

2. Davis, A. Y. *Women Race & Class.* Random House. New York, NY. 1983.

3. Boston, K. *Smart Money Moves for African Americans.* G.P. Putnam's Sons. New York, NY. 1996.

4. Ibid.

5. hooks, b. *Black Looks: Race and Representation.* South End Press. Boston, MA. 1992.

The Face of an Old Black Woman: Grandmothers and the Stability of Black Families

1. U. S. Census Bureau. Population Division, March 1998. Population Division Working Paper No. 26. *Co-resident Grandparents and Their Grandchildren: Grandparent Maintained Families.* Lynne M. Casper and Kenneth R. Bryson. Http://www.census.gov/population/www/documentation/twps0026/twps0026.html

2. Ibid.

3. Ibid.

Native American Women, Other Women, White Women

1. Hacker, A. *Two Nations Black and White, Separate, Hostile, Unequal.* Ballantine Books. New York, NY 1992.

2. hooks, b. *Killing Rage: Ending Racism.* Henry Holt & Company, Inc. New York, NY. 1995.

3. Ibid.

Myth of the "Ugly Body"

1. hooks, b. *Black Looks: Race and Representation.* South End Press. Boston, MA. 1992.

2. Ibid.

3. Ibid.

4. Rifkin, J. *The End of Work.* G. P. Putnam's Sons. New York, NY. 1995.

5. Latifah, Q. *Ladies First: Revelations of a Strong Woman.* William Morrow and Company, Inc. New York, NY. 1999.

6. Dixon, B. M., and Wilson, J. *Good Health for African Americans.* Crown Publishers, Inc. New York, NY. 1994.

7. Ibid.

8. Ibid.

9. Newsweek. September 27, 1999. *Shaped By Life In The Womb.* Begley, S.

10. Davis, J. C. A Woman's Special Health Needs. Delicious! Online http://www.healthwell.com/delicious-online/ D_Backs/Oct_97/woman.cfm

11 Dixon, B. M. and Wilson, J. *Good Health for African Americans.* Crown Publishers, Inc. New York, NY. 1994.

12. Ibid.

Part Three: Agencies and Institutions

Zero Tolerance for Black Skin: African American Women Behind Bars

1. U.S. Department of Justice Bureau of Justice Statistics. Victim Characteristics. March 21, 2000. http://www.ojp.usdoj.gov/bjs/cvict_v.htm

2. U.S. Department of Justice Bureau of Justice Statistics. August 12, 1998. Female Victims of Violent Crime. http://www.ojp.usdoj.gov/bjs/abstract/fvvc.htm

3. U.S. Department of Justice Bureau of Justice Statistics. Victim Characteristics. March 21, 2000. http://www.ojp.usdoj.gov/bjs/cvict_v.htm

4. Ebony. June 2000. *The Shocking Plight of Black Women Prisoners*. Davis, K.

5. News Briefs. Female Prison Population Grew 75%--1986 to 1991. August 1994. http://www.ndsn.org/AUGUST94/FEMALE.html

6. U.S. Department of Justice Bureau of Justice Statistics. Summary findings on December 31, 1999. Http://www.ojp.usdoj.gov/bjs/prisons.htm

The Political Pimping of Women

1. Davis, A. Y. *Women, Race & Class*. Random House. New York, NY. 1983.

2. Day, P. J. *A New History of Social Welfare*. Prentice Hall. Englewood Cliffs, NJ. 1989.

Educated to Become a White Man

1. Sadker, M. and Sadker, D. *Failing at Fairness: How Our Schools Cheat Girls.* TouchStone. New York, NY. 1994.

2. Day, P. J. *A New History of Social Welfare, Second Edition.* Allyn & Bacon. Needham Heights, MA. 1997.

Social Welfare and Women

1. Day, P. J. *A New History of Social Welfare, Second Edition.* Allyn and Bacon. Needham Heights, MA. 1997.

2. Ibid.

3. Ibid.

4. Ibid.

5. Wilson, A. N. *Awakening the Natural Genius of Black Children.* Afrikan World Infosystems. Bronx, NY. 1992.

Religion, *Men*-isters, and Women

1. Ani, M. *Yurugu: An African-Centered Critique of European Cultural Thought and Behavior.* Africa World Press, Inc. Trenton, NJ. 1994.

2. Ibid.

3. Ibid.

4. Ibid.

5. Diop, C. A. *The African Origin of Civilization Myth or Reality.* Lawrence Hill Books. Chicago, IL. 1983.

Part Four: The Wicked, the Mad, and the Spiritual

The Necessity of Female Rebellion

1. hooks, b. *Killing Rage: Ending Racism.* Henry Holt & Company, Inc. New York, NY. 1995.

2. Ibid.

Recommendations

What the Sisters Have to Say

1. Alpha Kappa Alpha Sorority, Incorporated. http://www.aka1908.com/boule_ty.htm

2. Delta Sigma Theta Sorority, Incorporated. http://www. dst1913.org/september/delta_academy. htm. 2000.

3. National Black Women's Health Project - About us. http://www.blackfamilies.com/community/groups/ WomensHealth/About_us.html

4. Ibid.

5. Welsing, F. C. *The Isis Papers: The Keys to the Colors.* Third World Press. Chicago, IL. 1991.

6. Ani, M. *Yurugu: An African-Centered Critique of European Cultural Thought and Behavior.* Africa World Press, Inc. Trenton, NJ. 1994.

7. Ibid.

8. Ibid.

9. Dixon, B. M., and Wilson, J. *Good Health for African Americans.* Crown Publishers, Inc. New York, NY. 1994.

10. Ani, M. *Yurugu: An African-Centered Critique of European Cultural Thought and Behavior.* Africa World Press, Inc. Trenton, NJ. 1994.